…

Loom Jewelry for B

An Illustrated Step By

By Melinda Rolf.

A Home Life Book

All Rights Reserved. No part of this publication may be reproduced in any form or by any means, including scanning, photocopying, or otherwise without prior written permission of the copyright holder. Copyright © 2014 eQuivia Books™

Rainbow Loom®

So you have discovered the Rainbow Loom® craze that is sweeping the nation? It is so much fun! These are easy to follow, easy to learn patterns so play around, get comfortable and remember to try lots of different colors that will show off your personality.

Before you dive into the fun of making your own super cool bracelets, backpack tags and keychains, here are some fun facts about the Rainbow Loom® that you may not know.

- *The Rainbow Loom® was invented in 2010 by Cheong Choon Ng from Novi, Michigan.*
- *The Loom measures 2 inches by 8 inches.*
- *The knots that are made when looping the bands are called Brunnian Links.*
- *As of September 2013 over 1.2 million looms have been sold*
- *Some schools have banned Rainbow Looms® as they say the children are distracted from their studies.*
- *Rainbow Loom® is a finalist in three categories in this years' "Toy of the Year" contest.*
- *Rainbow Loom® bracelets make great friendship bracelets*
- *And here's some good news for Moms and Dads. Some therapists believe that making loom bracelets and other items can "Improve visual and perceptual skills and help with problem solving, finger dexterity, hand strength, coordination and more". Source: Occupational Therapist, Jennifer Todd-Barnard.*
-

In this book you will find simple and easy to follow along Instructions that will have you on your way to creating your very own super cool bracelets, backpack tags, key chains and more. Each project gives step by step Instructions: with images so you can follow along and know you are doing it right.

Simple Rainbow Chain Bracelet

I have put together a few tips and ideas that hopefully will make your new hobby a more fun and enjoyable experience

- It's a good idea to have all your supplies ready before you start your project. Have all your bands organized by color and make sure you have enough to complete the project.
- Try to work on a flat surface. A desk or kitchen table is perfect as you will need some space to work and have all your supplies close at hand.
- If you are not the most organized person, you can buy plastic cases at Michaels to keep your bands in
- You can also buy (or make) a chart like a table with squares saying XYZ or ABC This is where you can put your bands while you are working. This will help if you want to use different colors than the ones in the Instructions.

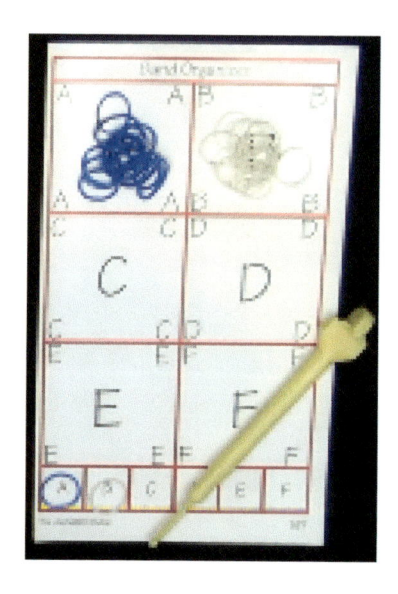

- Try to finish the project you are working on before you start a new one.
- Don't be afraid to ask for help if you make a mistake, start to get lost or feel frustrated. Your mom, Dad or siblings might be able to show you how to get back on track.
- Take a break! Don't sit at the kitchen table for hours and hours. Go outside for a while, or have a snack break. You will come back with fresh eyes and will feel much better about continuing on.

HAVE FUN

CONTENTS	PAGE
The So Simple Spiral	6
The Super-Cool Backpack Tag	17
The Simple Rainbow	25
The Trendy Triple Single	31
The Easy-Peasy Key Chain	41
The Fabulous Four-Pin Fishtail	48
The Must-Have Honeycomb	54
The Super Single Rhombus	65
The Fishtail Friendship Necklace	74
The Super Hip Headband	78

NOTE: The corresponding images are always below the Instructions:

So Simple Spiral Bracelet

Hint:

Keep your hook vertical and slightly tilted forward

You will need:

Loom

Hook

C-clip

13 color bands of your choice (X) I am using green

12 color bands of your choice (Y) I am using white

Some extra bands to make the extension

Instructions:

Hint: It is a good idea to use the same colors as in the Instructions: until you have made a couple of bracelets or other items.

Place the loom so that the arrows are pointing away from you. Place your (Y) band (mine is white) from the center pin to the 1st pin on the left.

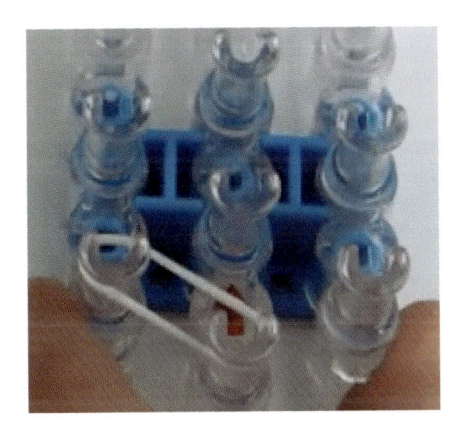

Now take your (X) band (mine is green) and place it from the center pin to the 2nd pin on the left.

Take your (Y) band (mine is white) and place it from the 1st pin on the left to the 2nd center pin.

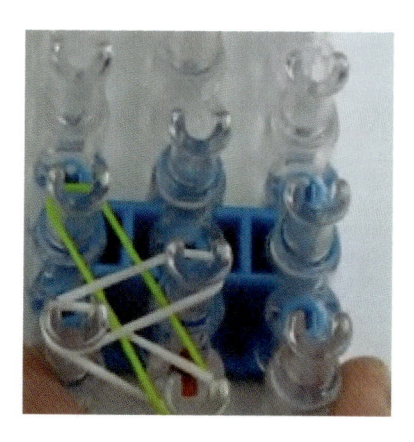

Now you want to alternate the colors so take your (Y) band (mine is white) and place it from the 2nd center pin to the 3rd left pin.

Take your (X) band (mine is green) and place it from the next left pin to the next center pin.

Continue this same pattern (white green, green white, white green, green white) all the way down the loom. You will finish on the center pin.

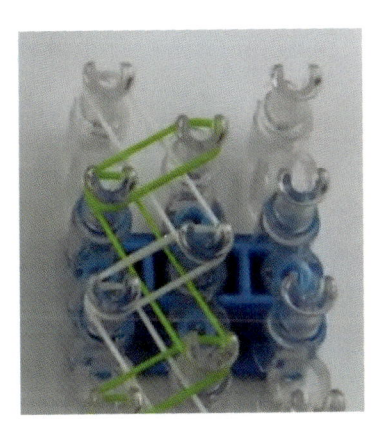

Now take one of your (X) bands (mine is green) double it up and place it over the top left pin. It should be going over your (Y) color band (mine is white)

Now turn the loom around so that the arrows are pointing towards you.

It's time to start looping

At the first pin on the right side, put your hook in the hole and push back your (X) bands (mine are green) and grab the (Y) band (mine is white) and place it on the 2nd center pin.

Now take the band on the front center pin and place it on the 2nd right pin.

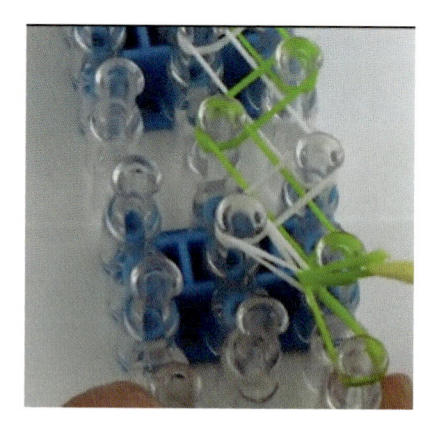

At that same pin, (2nd right) grab the bottom band (mine is green) and place it on the next center pin (3rd)

At that same pin (2nd center) grab the bottom band (mine is white) and place it on the next right pin (3rd)

Continue this same pattern all the way down the loom (you should be putting the same color bands on top of the same color bands) (green on green, white on white, white on white green on green, green on green, white on white etc.).Your colors may be different but that is the pattern. You will finish at the bottom center pin. It should look the image below.

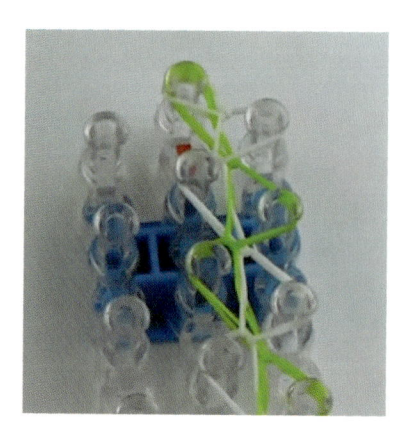

Now put your hook through the hole at the front center pin and push it out of the space on the left (see picture below)

Attach a (Y) band (mine is white) to the hook and carefully pull it through the bands holding the other end with two fingers Put both ends onto the hook and push them down to the thick part of the hook.

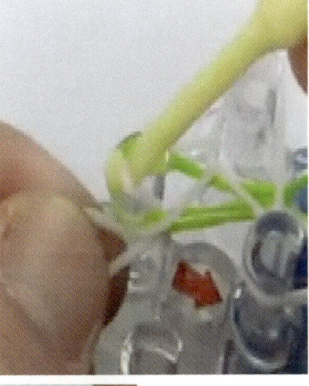

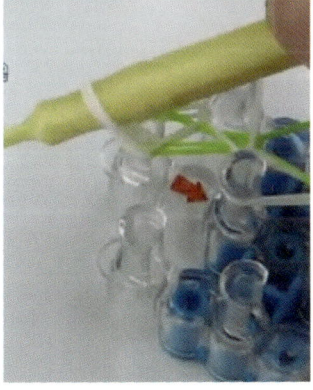

You can now carefully remove the bands from the loom.

Time to make the extension

Turn the loom around so that the arrows are pointing away from you. Take your "extra" bands and alternating the colors, place them down the pins on the right of the loom (4 to 6 bands depending on the size of your wrist)

13

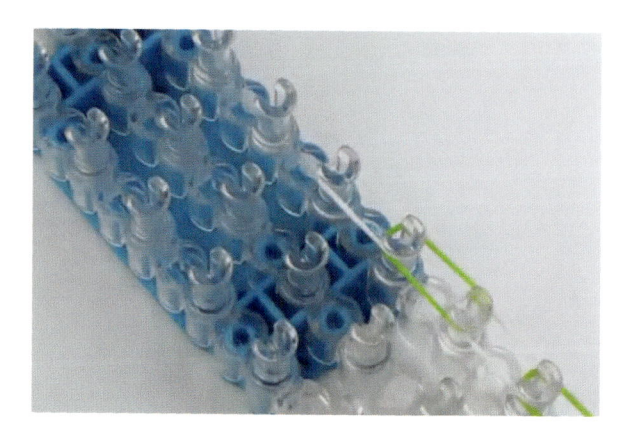

Now take your loom and remove the bracelet. Stretch the bands on the end over the last pin that you placed your extension on, to the pin in front.

Turn the loom so that the arrows are now pointing towards you. Starting at the second pin on the left, hook your band and place it on the pin in front.

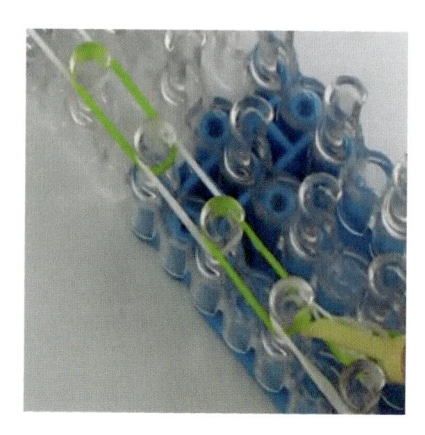

Now hook the band on that pin (it should be a different color) and place it on the pin in front.

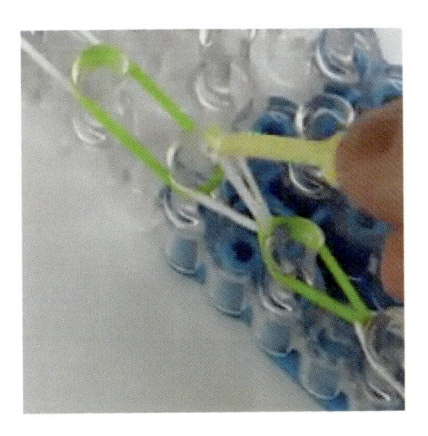

Continue this down the loom to the last band of your extension. Take your C-clip and attach it to the last band of your extension on the left side.

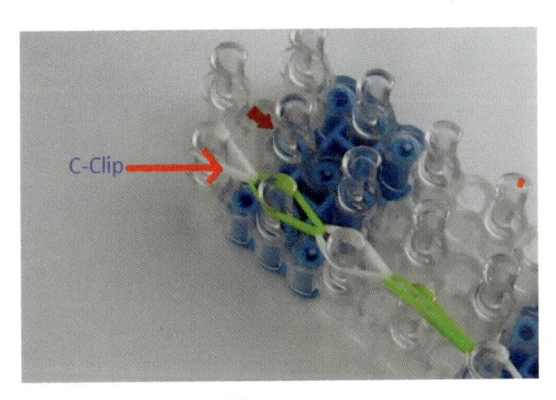

Holding the C-clip, remove the extension from the loom and attach the double bands at the other end to the C-clip.

Way to go! You just finished the "So-Simple-Spiral" Bracelet

Super-Cool Backpack Tag

You will need:

Loom

Hook

54 bands-your choice of color, I will use green) X

24 bands of a different color, (I will use grey) Y

11 bands of a different color, (I will use white) Z

C-clip

Keychain

Instructions:

Place the loom with the red arrows pointing away from you. (Notice the curved side of the pins. This is where you will place your bands) Take 2 of your first color bands...(X) (my green) and place them both from the front center, to the 1st pin on the left. Then continue placing 2 bands all the way down the left side and stop and the 2nd to last pin. It should like the image below (except with your choice of color bands)

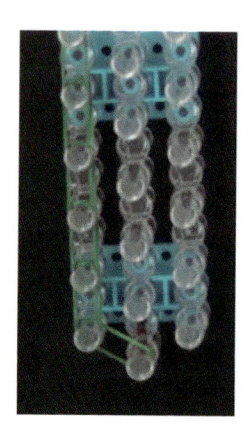

When you get to the 2nd to last pin on the left, place 2 bands from the left pin to the pin in the center.

Go back to the front of the loom and do the same thing down the right side of the loom starting center pin to 1st pin on the right (always using 2 bands at a time and using the same colors as on the left side) Again stop at 2nd to last and hook from there to the center pin. Go back to the front of the loom.

Now chose your second color of bands (Y) (mine are grey) and starting from the front center pin, place 2 of your 2nd color bands all the way down the center row of pins The last 2 bands will end on the front center pin. Now push all the bands down the pins and go back to the front of the loom.

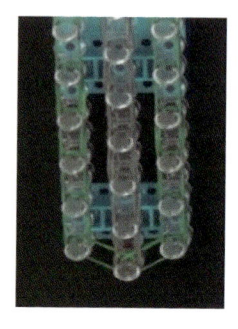

Now it's time to use your remaining colored bands. (Z) Mine are white. Take one band and starting at the 2nd center pin, make a triangle from the 2nd center pin to the pins on the right and left.

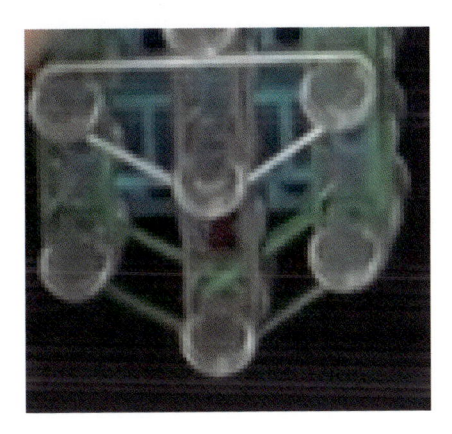

Do the same thing all the way down the loom. It should look like the image below.

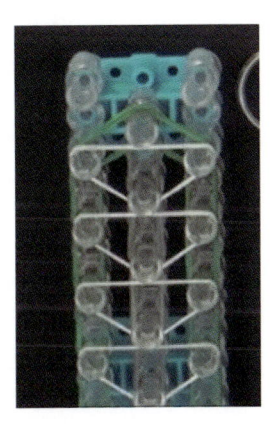

It's time to start looping.

Turn your loom around so the arrow is now pointing towards you. Go to the other end of the loom. On the front center pin (the one with your 1st color band, place your key ring (or backpack tag)

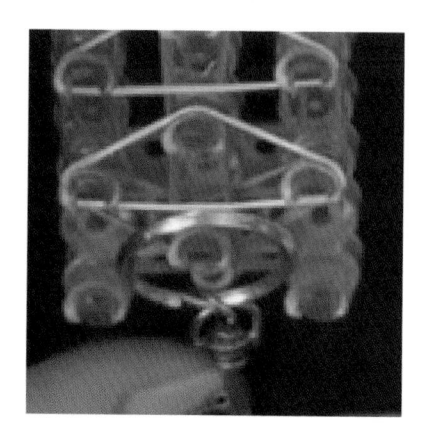

Take your hook and put it into the front center hole and grab the bands you used 2nd (Z).. (mine are grey) and pull them up and over the keychain ring and onto the pin in front (2nd center pin)

Do the same at the 2nd center pin, (put your hook into the hole, grab the "grey (Y)" bands and hook them up and over to the pin in front. Continue down the center row) When done, go back to the other end of the loom. It should look like the image below.

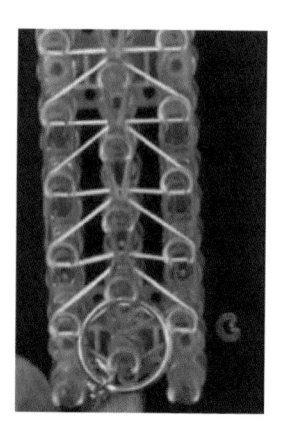

Now put your hook into the hole at the first center pin and grab the top two 1st colored bands (X) (mine are green) and hook them onto the first pin on the left.

Now, very carefully using the back of your loom stick, push back all the bands on this pin, (including the "triangle" (Z) band, mine is white) except the bottom two 1st color (X) bands (mine are green), grab those bottom two bands, lift them up and over and place them on the pin in front (2nd left). See image below.

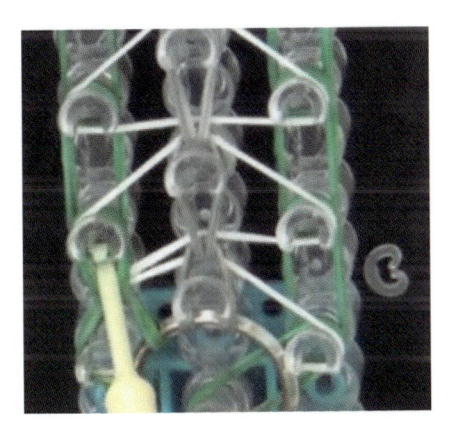

Make sure to hook both bands. (You might want to secure the other bands with your thumb) Do this all the way down the left row of the loom ending by placing them on the center pin. (The triangle shape should stay intact)

Go back to the front of the loom where the keychain ring is, and at the center pin, grab the bands and place them on the 1st right pin.

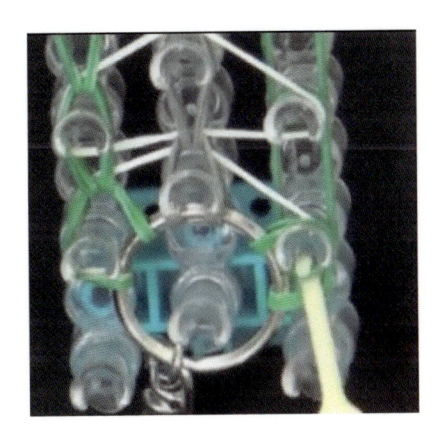

Continue down the right row of the loom and be sure to push back the triangle band before you grab the bands. Finish by looping the last one to the center pin. It should look like this.

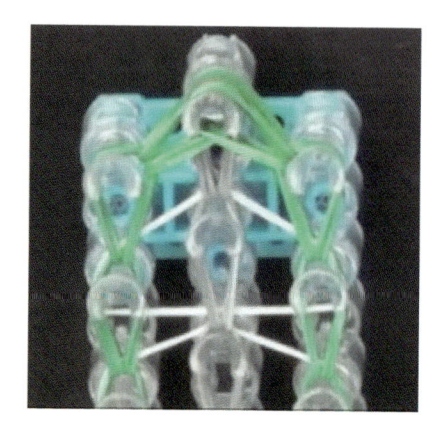

Now at the last center pin where you just placed the bands, pull all of the bands up to the top of the pin Put your hook into the space at the front and out of the space on the left side of the loom (see image below) Make sure all the bands are around the hook.

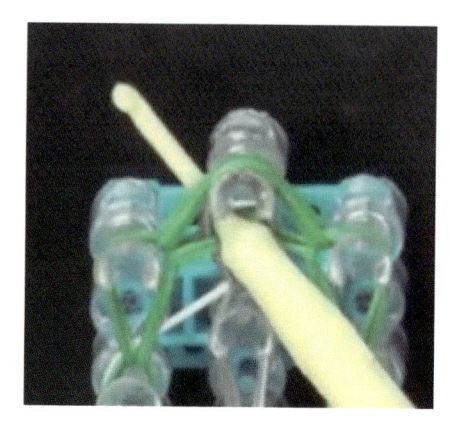

Now take 2 of your (X) colored bands, mine are green, and place them on the end of the hook.

Carefully pull the hook and the band back through the space.

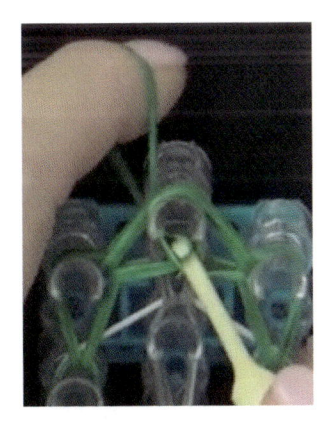

Place the other end of the bands (the ones around your finger), onto the hook and slide them down to the thick part of the hook. You can now carefully remove the bands from the loom. Attach a C-clip to the band around the hook Remove the bands.

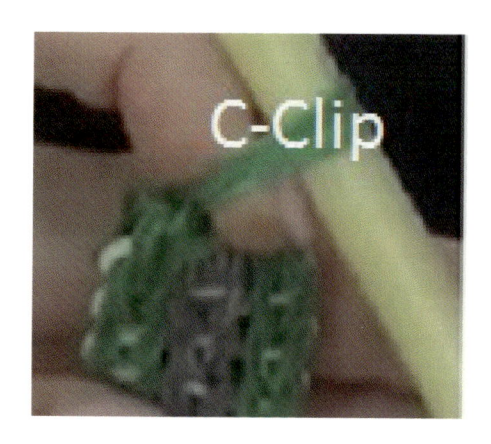

Congratulations, your super cool backpack tag is finished

Super Simple Rainbow-Chain Bracelet

You will need:

Loom

Hook

13 red bands

12 yellow bands

C-clip to attach the two ends together

Remember, you can use any band colors that you choose. Just be careful to match the colors with the Instructions:

Instructions:

Place the loom with the red arrows pointing away from you. (Notice the curved side of the pins. This is where you will place your bands)

Hint:

When placing the band on the pins, stretch the band a little further than the pin and then let it go

Starting at the front center pin, place a red band around that pin and stretch it from that pin to the 1st pin on the right side of the loom. Push the band down.

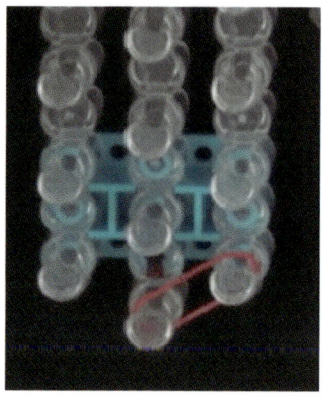

Take a yellow band and place it over the pin on the right where you just put the red band. Stretch it to the 2nd pin in the center row of the loom.

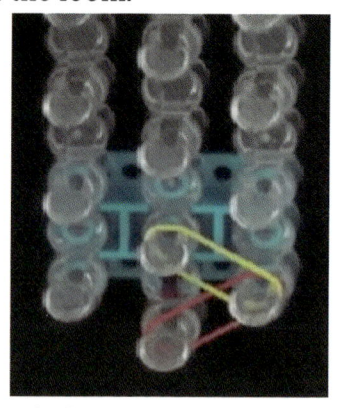

Take a red band and place it on the same pin (2nd pin center row) and stretch it to the 2nd pin on the right.

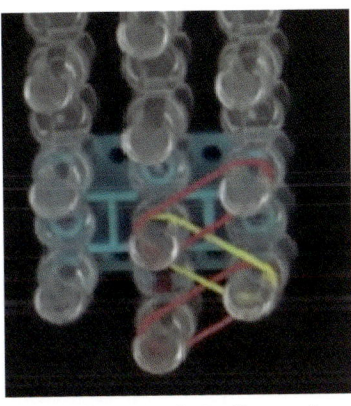

Take a yellow band and stretch it from that pin on the right to the next pin (3rd) in the center Continue this pattern (alternating colors) all the way down to the end of the loom (right to center, center to right) Remember to push the bands down each time.

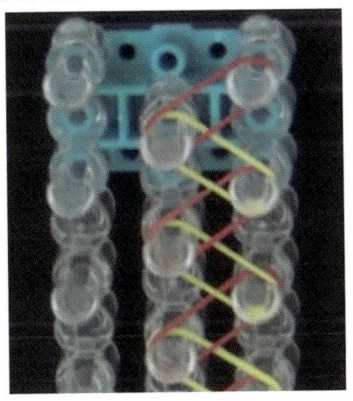

Once you reach the end, turn the loom around so now the red arrow is pointing towards you.

Steady the loom with your left hand, take your hook with the open part facing up and push down the red band on the first center hook and hook the yellow band underneath.

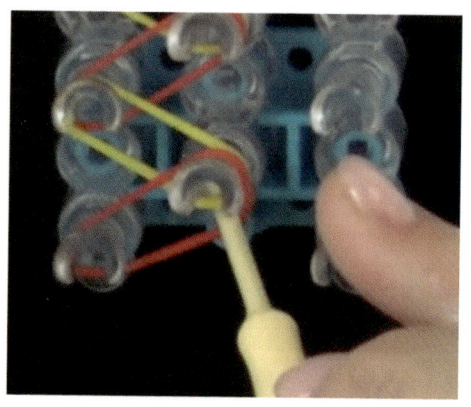

Carefully remove the yellow band off the pin and stretch it to the 2nd pin on the left side of the loom.

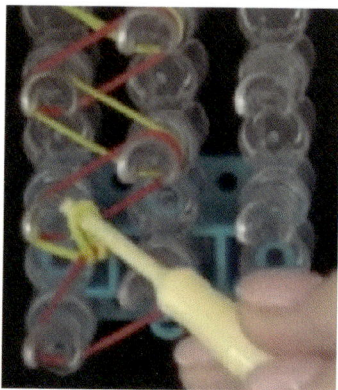

Push down on the bands on the 2nd pin on the left side and hook the red band. Stretch it to the 2nd pin in the center.

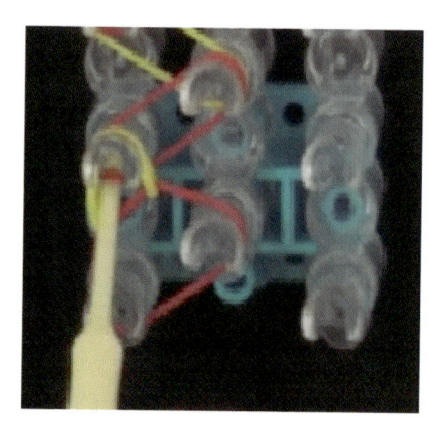

Now push down on the bands on that pin (2nd center) and hook the bottom band (yellow) and stretch it to the 3rd pin on the left.

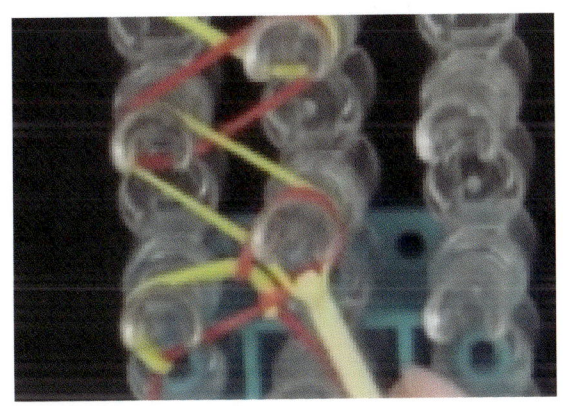

Do this all the way down the loom. (You can tell which pin you just used as the bands will make a teardrop shape on the pin) Keep hooking the last band on the pin and stretching it over from left to middle from middle to left. The last band will be from the left to the middle (the pin on its own at the back of the loom)

Now pull the last red band and stretch it to the pin on the right side of the loom.

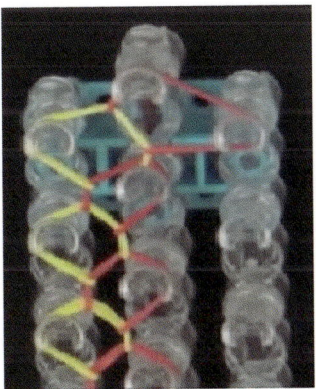

Take your C-clip and attach it to the red band at the top right of the loom (the part that stretches from the top middle to the top right)

29

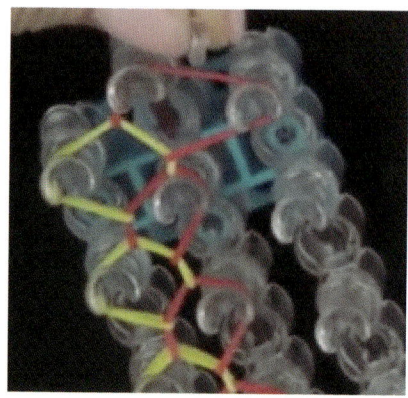

Once the C-clip is attached, slowly and carefully remove the bands from the loom keeping hold of the band with the C-clip.

Once it is removed, double up the band at the other end and attach it to the C-clip. Your bracelet is now ready to wear.

Good Job! You just made a simple rainbow bracelet

The Trendy Triple Single Bracelet

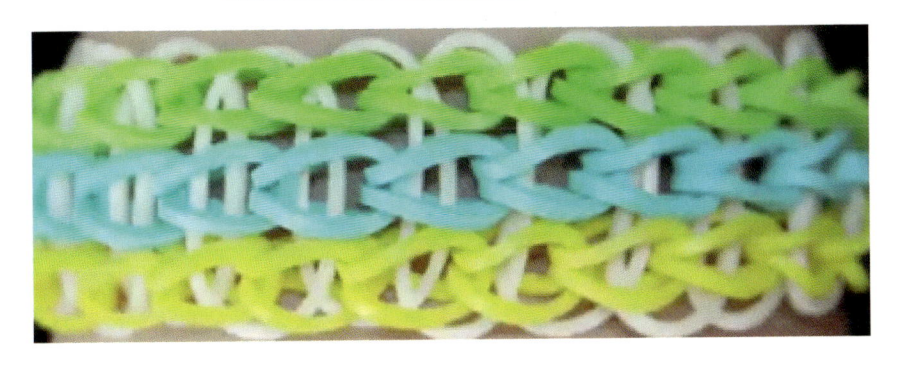

You will need:

Loom

Hook

13 (W) bands (I am using green)

14 (X) bands I am using blue

13 (Y) bands I am using yellow

10 (Z) bands I am using white

C-clip to attach the two ends together

Instructions:

> Place the loom with the red arrows pointing away from you. (Notice the curved side of the pins. This is where you will place your bands)
>
> Stretch a green band or your own color) from the front center pin to the 1st left pin Push the band down.
>
> Place a band on top of the green band on the left pin and stretch it to the 2nd pin on the left.

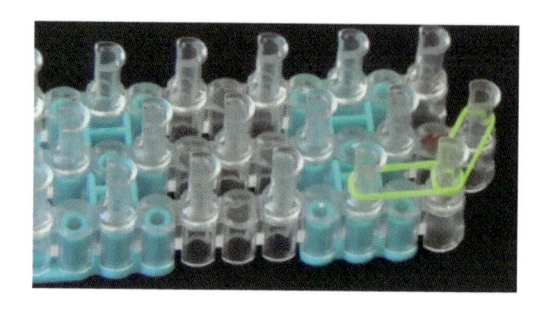

Do this all the way down the left side of the loom until you reach the pin that is the last one on the left below the center back pin. Put the last green band from this pin to the center back pin.

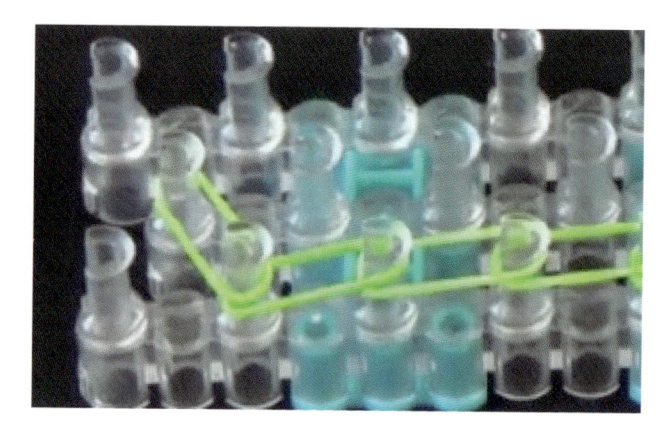

Go back to the front of the loom and place a row of blue bands from the front center all the way down the middle to the center back pin.

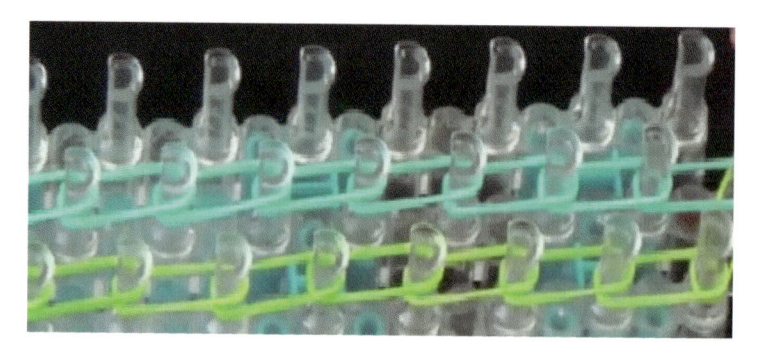

Go back to the front and place a yellow band from the front center to 1st right.

Right side

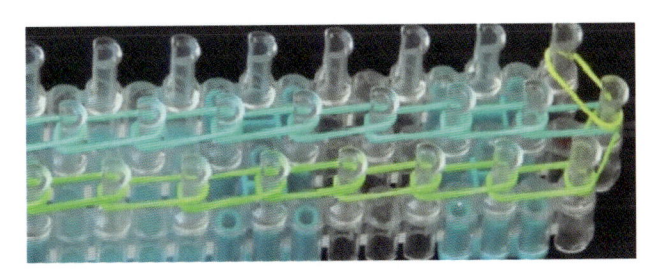

Then place yellow bands all the way down the right side of the loom to the back center pin.

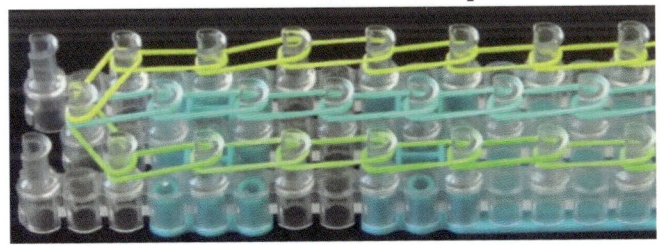

Take a blue band, double it and put it on the back center pin, push it down.

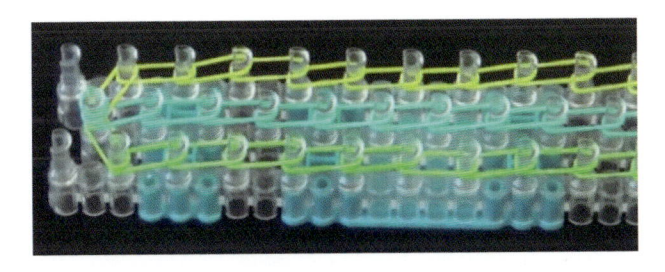

Go back to the front and stretch a white band over the 2nd set of three pins (right center and left) It should look like a triangle with the front of the triangle on the center pin.

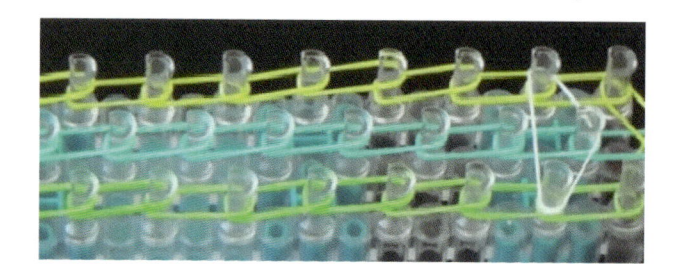

Do this all the way down the loom. You should have 10 triangles when done (Don't go as far as the bottom center pin)

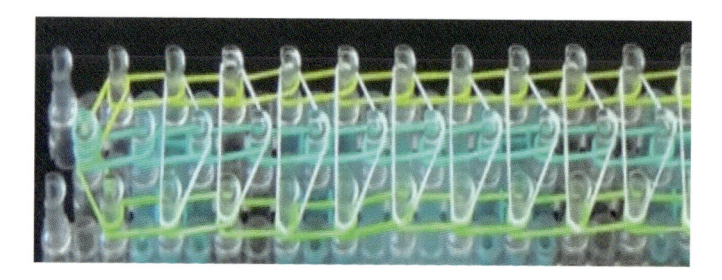

It's time to start looping

Turn your loom around so that the arrows are now pointing towards you Take your hook with the open part of the hook facing up and the flat side of the hook facing down.

On the center pin and using the back of the hook, push the double blue band out of the way so you can grab the yellow band and pull it up through the center of the blue band.

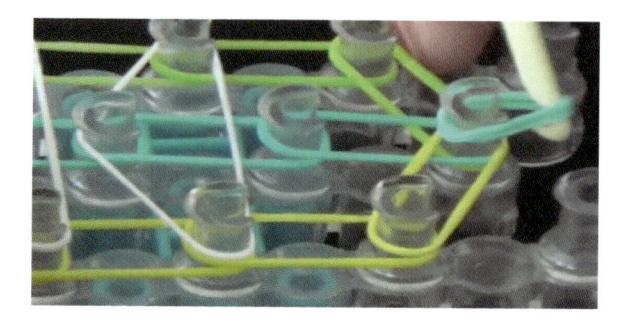

(You might want to use your thumb to hold the blue band in place so it doesn't come off the pin) then stretch the yellow band over to the pin on the left.

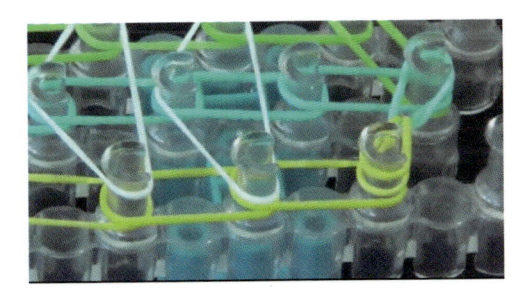

Now take your hook and carefully go into the pin on the left and pushing back the top 2 yellow bands, grab the bottom part of the yellow band and bring it up the center of the pin then over (off) the pin and hook it to the pin in front (it should now be on top of the white band)

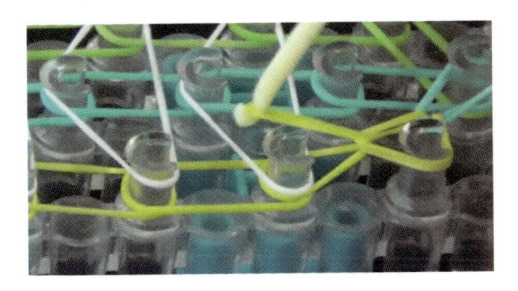

Now place your hook into this pin and pushing back the white band, grab the bottom yellow band and bring it up and over onto the pin in front.

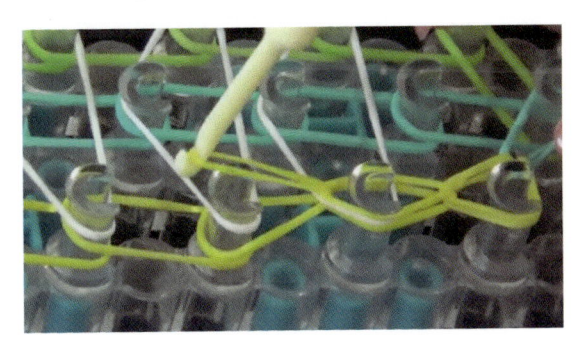

Do the same thing on this pin....push the white band back and grab the yellow, pull it up and over onto the pin in front. Continue all the way down the left side ending by stretching the last band from the left pin to the center pin at the end of the loom.

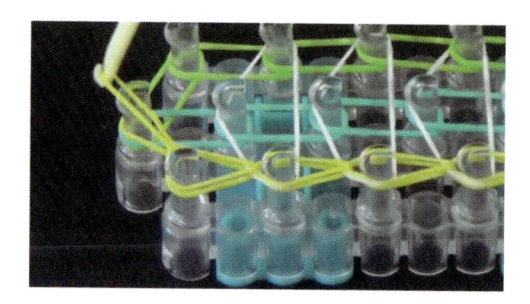

Go back to the front of the loom to the center row , pull the blue cap band back and hook the top blue band and lift it up and over onto the pin in front on the center row.

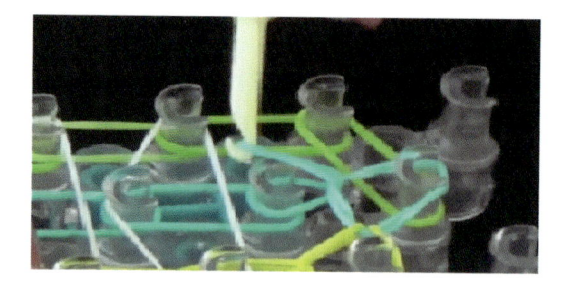

Continue pulling the blue band up and over all the way down the center row (There is no white band to pull back in the center row) Push all the bands down.

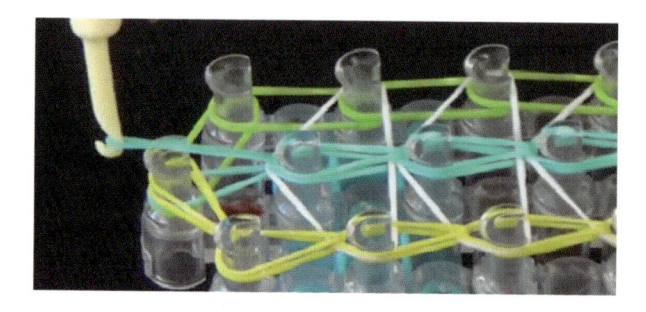

Go back to the front center pin, push back the blue cap band and hook the green band and loop it over onto the 1st pin on the right side of the loom.

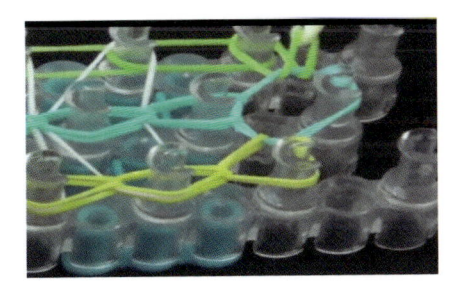

On the 1st right pin, reach into the teardrop shape and push back the top 2 green bands, grab the bottom green and pull it up and over onto the 2nd pin on the right.

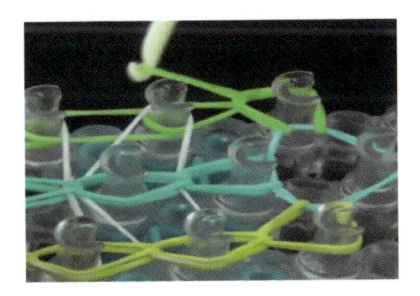

At the 2nd pin, you will do the same but this time you will have to push back the white triangle band in order to grab the green.

Continue down the right side of the loom ending by placing the green band on the back center pin.

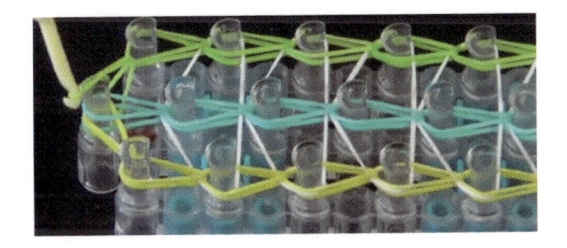

Time to finish the bracelet

Turn the loom around. On the top center pin, scrunch all the bands together to the top of the pin with your thumbs. Put your hook with the hook facing up, down the middle of the pin through all the bands and tilt it out through the space on the right.

Put a blue band on the hook and keeping a hold on it with your fingers, pull the blue band through the bands.

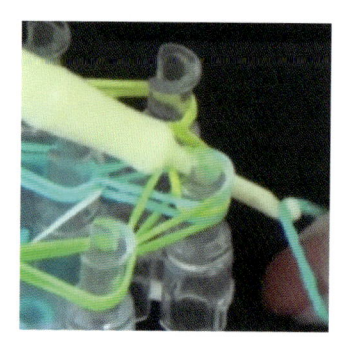

Then put both ends of the blue band over the hook and slide the blue band down to the thick part of the hook. Keeping hold of the hook, grab the band with the C-clip. You can now pull all the bands off the loom from front to back.

Extend the bracelet

Take blue bands and put them down the right side of the loom starting at the 1st pin on the right. Go down 4 or 6 pins depending on the size of your wrist.

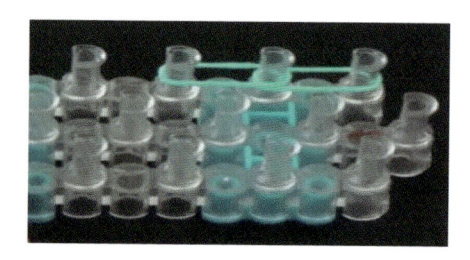

Now pick up your bracelet and open up the blue cap band that is attached on one end and stretch it over the last pin that you extended to, to the one in front.

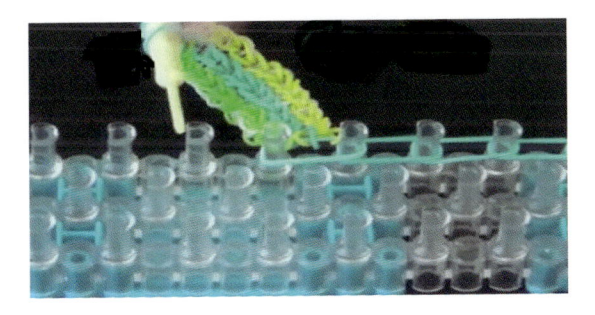

Now hook the blue band on the last pin you extended to and hook it to the pin behind (you are now going backwards towards the front of the loom) Pull the last one to the center pin.

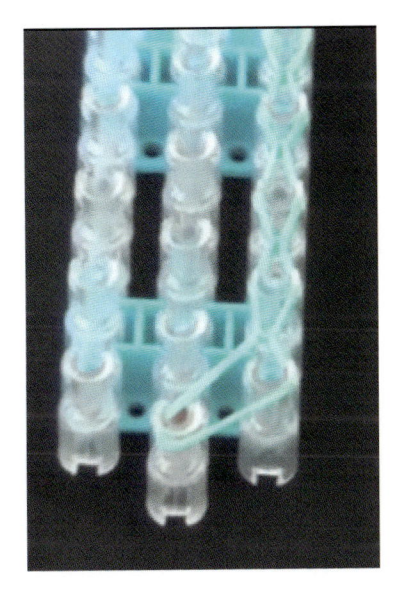

Now get your C-clip and put it over the bands on the front center pin.

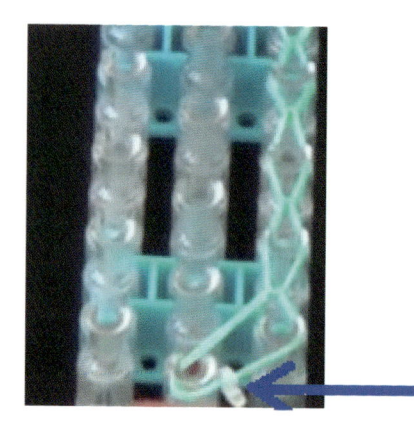

C-clip

Holding the band with the C-clip, take the bracelet off the loom Pull the band away from the hook so you can get your fingers in there. Take the band off the hook and onto your fingers. Stretch the bands with your fingers so that you can put the C-clip from the other end over the bands.

Congratulations, you just finished your triple single bracelet

Easy Peasy Key Chain

You will need:

Loom

Hook

13 black bands

3 of your favorite color bands (12 groups of colors) 36 bands in all

Instructions:

Place your loom with the arrows pointing away from you.

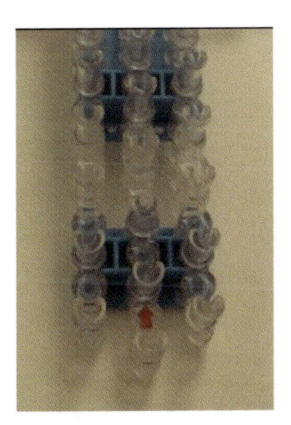

Take a black band and place it from the 1st center pin to the 2nd center pin. The take another black band and place it from the 2nd center pin to the 3rd center pin.

Continue this (2nd to 3rd, 3rd to 4th etc.) all the way down the center of the loom.

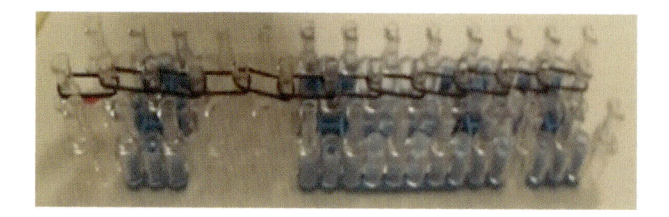

Push the bands down and go back to the front of the loom (arrow facing away)

Now take 3 of the same colored bands and stretch them from the front pin to the two pins on the right and left. It should make a triangle shape.

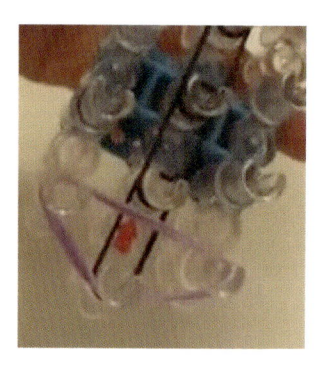

Now do the same thing with a group of 3 same colored bands (but a different color than the first ones) and make a triangle from the 2nd center pin to the 2nd pins on the right and left.

Continue this pattern all the way down the loom to the 2nd to last set of pins.

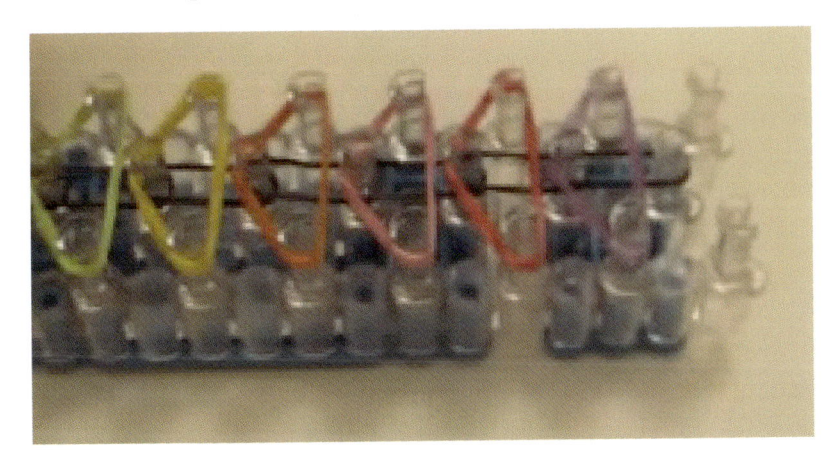

Now make a cap band by taking a black band and doubling it (make a figure 8 then bring it together) Place this double band over the last center pin.

Turn the loom so that the arrow is pointing towards you.

It's time to start looping!

Place your hook down the center of the first center pin and pushing the cap band out of the way, grab the black band underneath (be sure to hold the cap band in place with your thumb so it doesn't come off the pin) bring the black band up and off the pin and loop it onto the pin in front.

Now hook the colored band on the right side of the middle pin and take it off the center pin.

It should now look like this.

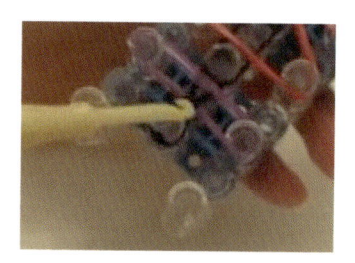

Next, put your hook in front of the colored band that you just removed, reach down and grab the black band and hook it onto the pin in front.

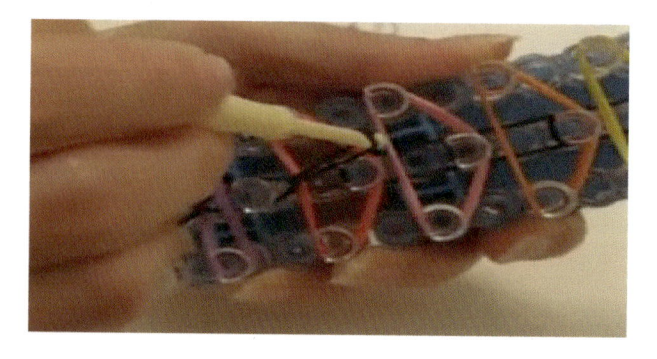

Once again grab the triangle band on the right of the front pin and take it off the pin.

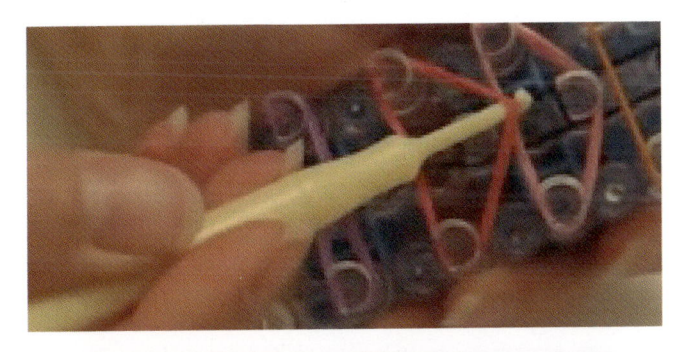

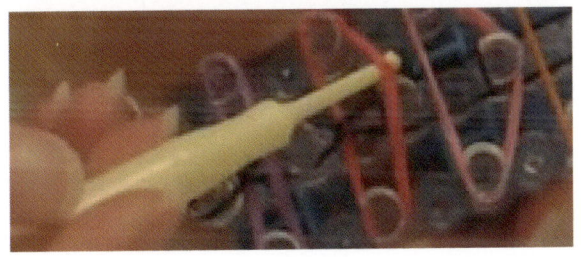

It should now look like the image below.

Now again, pushing the color band back, reach in and grab the black band and place it on the center pin in front. Then take the color band off the pin into the middle. Continue this down the loom.

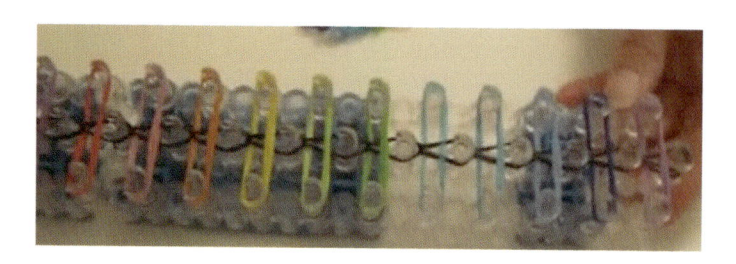

At the back of the loom where you just finished, put your hook down the center of the front center pin and out of the space in the side. Take a new black band and hook it onto the end of the hook. Then holding one end of the black band, pull it through the space and hook the other end (that you have in your fingers) onto the hook.

Holding your hook with the black band over it, gently pull the bands off the loom. Now slide the black bands to the end of the hook. Take the black band at the back and pull it over the front band and off the hook. Then pull it tight.

Well done! You just made the Easy Peasy Keychain

The Fabulous Four-Pin Fishtail

You will need:
Loom
Hook
12 black bands
24 white bands (Have a few extra of all the bands just in case)
24 grey bands
C-clip

Instructions:

(Hint)
Push down all the bands each time you complete an action

NOTE: For this bracelet, You will need to take the center row of pins, remove it then put it back so that the front pins are all lined up with each other (The arrows should be on your left and pointing to the right) You will only work with the bottom right 4 pins)

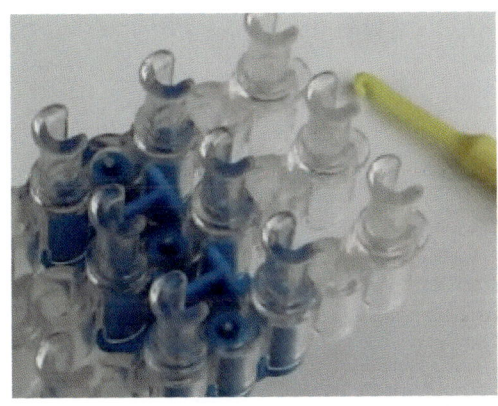

Take a black band and place it around all the 4 pins (see image)

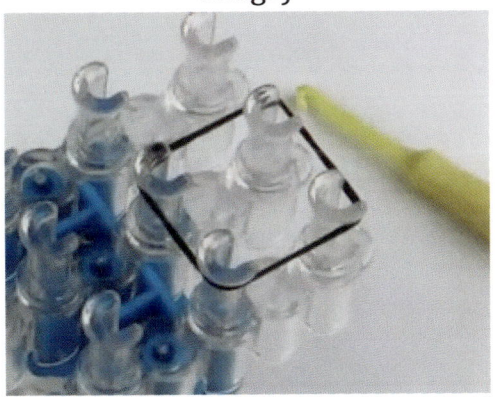

Take your hook and grab a C-clip. Put the C-clip on one side of the bands. Now using your hook, attach the other 3 sides of the bands to the C-clip. Push the bands down.

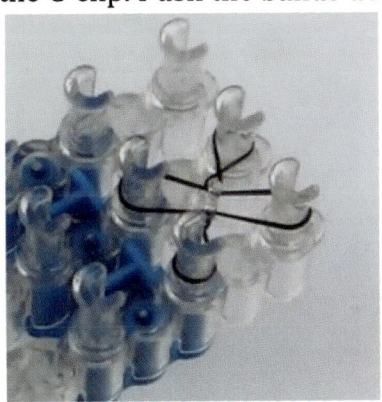

Now take a grey band and place it round all 4 pins just like you did with the black one.

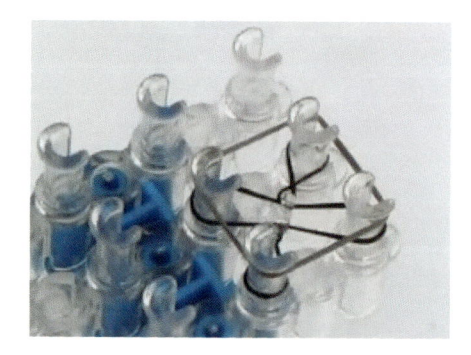

Grab the black band from the front left pin, (under the grey) pull it up & over the gray band and the pin and release it.

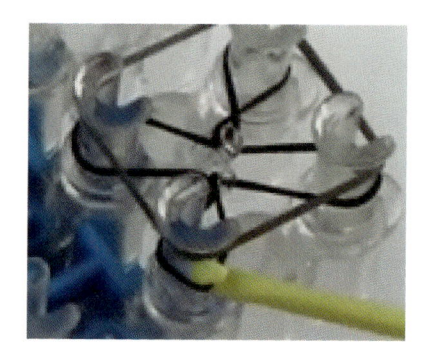

Do the same thing on the other 3 pins. Push the bands down. It should look like the image below.

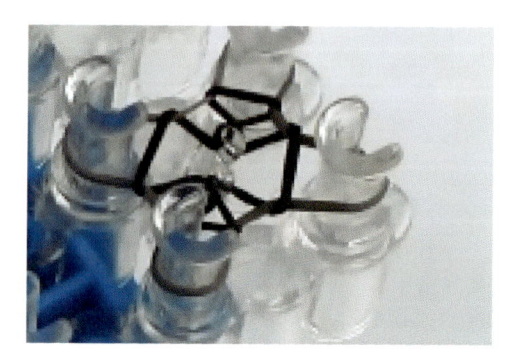

Now put on a white band and repeat what you just did (pull the band over and release)

Keep repeating using this sequence.

White

White

Grey

Black

Grey

White

White

Grey

Black

Grey

Keep repeating.

The bands will start to come out of the bottom of the loom. You can pull it down gently.

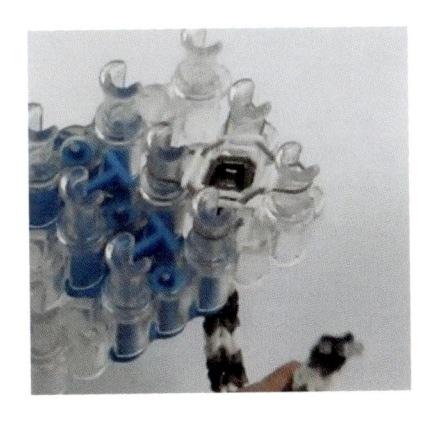

Keep going until your bracelet is at the length you want it.

Now take the other end of the bracelet and push all the bands on the C-clip to one side and hold the C-clip like in the image below.

Now while still holding the C-clip, place your hook into the top left pin and grab the band (see image below)

Take the grey band off the pin and onto the hook.

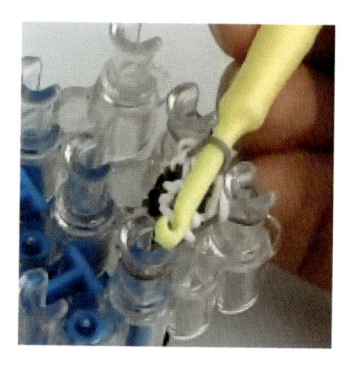

Now place your hook into the bottom left pin and grab the grey band onto the hook.

Do the same with the other two pins so that all 4 bands are on the hook, then hook the C-clip from the other end onto all 4 bands on the loom (if this is hard, you might want to ask someone to help) Take the bracelet off the hook and.........

You have just made The Fabulous Four-Pin Fishtail

Once you get good at this, replace the white bands with "glow in the dark" bands for a super cool look.

The Must-Have Honeycomb Bracelet

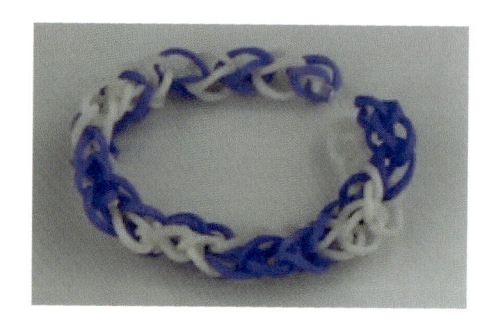

You will need:

Loom

Hook

12 color bands of your choice (I am using blue)

13 color bands of your choice (I am using white)

C-clip

Extra bands for the extension

Instructions:

Place the loom so that the arrows are pointing away from you

Place a blue band from the front center pin to the 1st pin on the left.

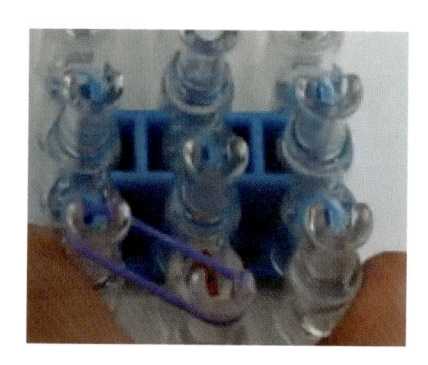

Now place a white band from the center pin to the 1st pin on the right.

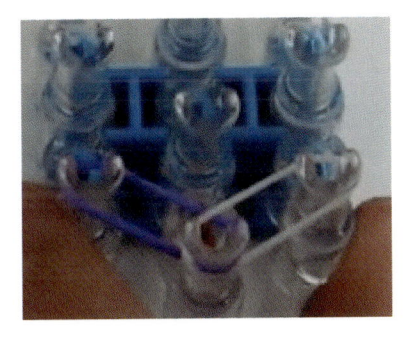

Now take a blue band and place it from the 1st left pin to the pin in front.

Do the same with a white band on the other side (1st right to pin one in front)

Place a blue band from the 2nd pin on the left to the 3rd center pin.

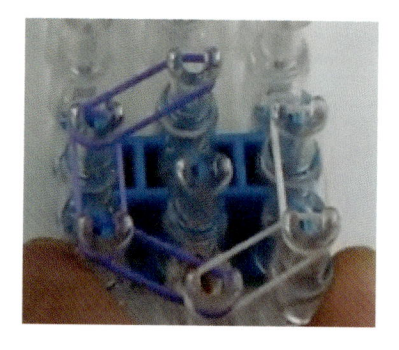

And place a white band from 2nd right pin to 3rd center pin. This should make a honeycomb shape (hexagon)

Now place a white band from the 3rd center to the 3rd left.

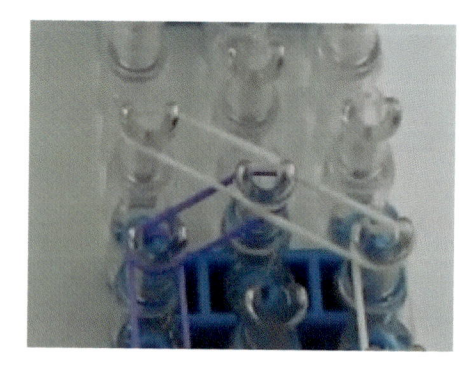

Now continue with a blue from 3rd center to 3rd right.

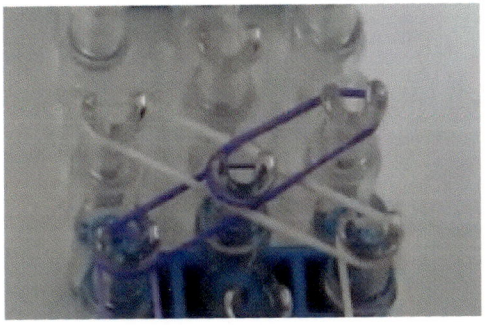

Now place a white band from 3rd left to 4th left and a blue band from 3rd right to 4th right.

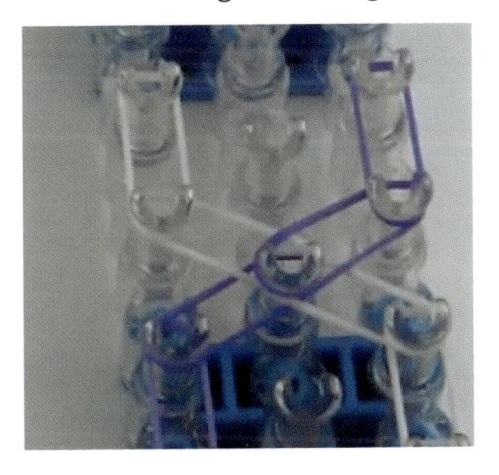

Then a white from 4th left to center and a blue from 4th right to center.

(Hint)

There should always be an empty center pin each time as you make the hexagon shape

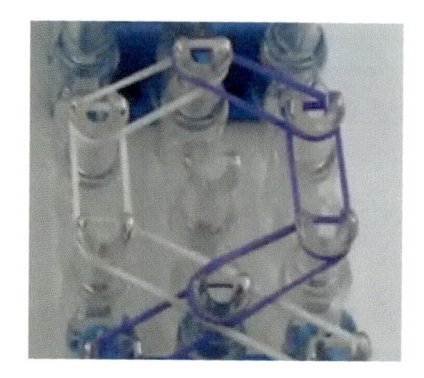

Now continue this pattern all the way down the loom remembering to alternate the colors on each side.

When you get to the front center pin, double up a white band and put it on that pin.

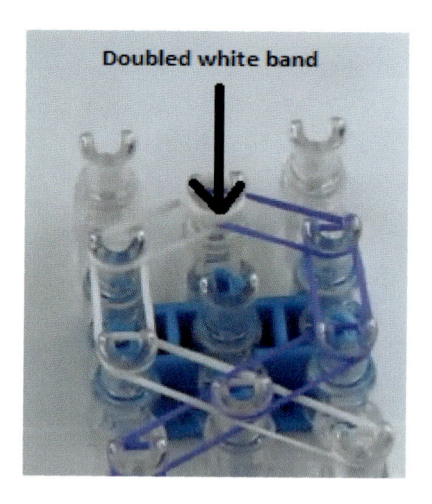

Turn the loom around so that the arrows are pointing towards you.

It's time to start looping!

Start at the front center pin and pushing back the white band, grab the blue band and hook it up and off the pin and put it on top of the other bands on the 2nd left pin.

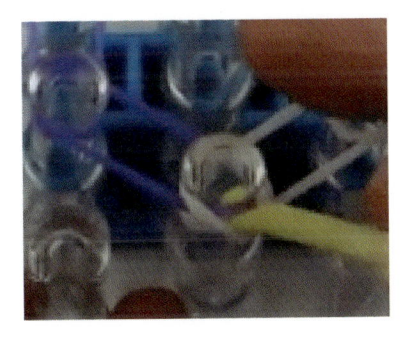

Then at the same pin (center) Push back the top white, grab the bottom white and put it on the 2nd right on top of the other white bands (see image below)

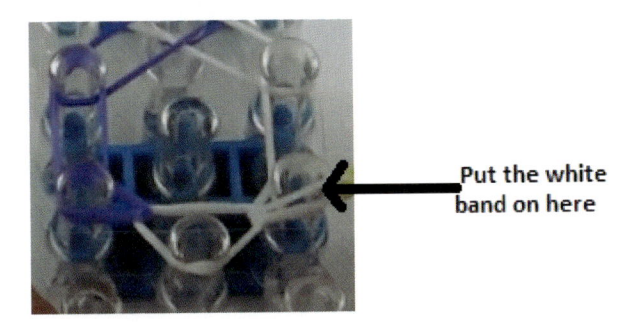

Put the white band on here

Now go back to the 2nd left pin, grab the bottom blue band and hook it onto the pin in front. Do the same on the right.

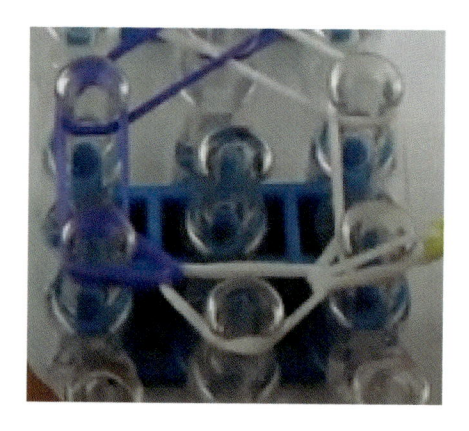

Then take the blue band from left 3 and put it on the center pin and do the same with the white band on the right.

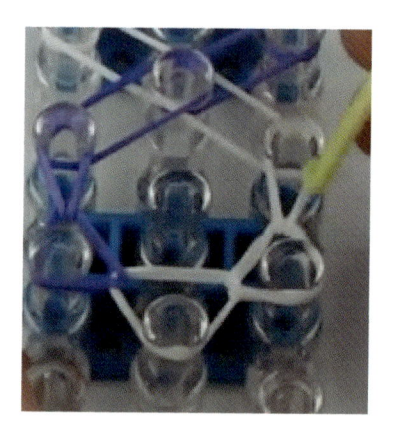

Continue this pattern at each honeycomb (Center to left, center to right, left to left in front, right to right in front, left to center, right to center) do this all the way down the loom, ending at the front center pin.

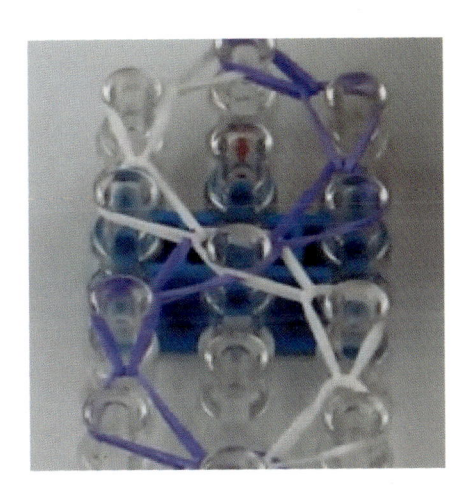

Now put your hook through the bands in the top center pin and out the other side. Holding one end of the band with your fingers, carefully pull it through the pin hole and attach the end of the band you are holding onto the hook. Push the band down the hook.

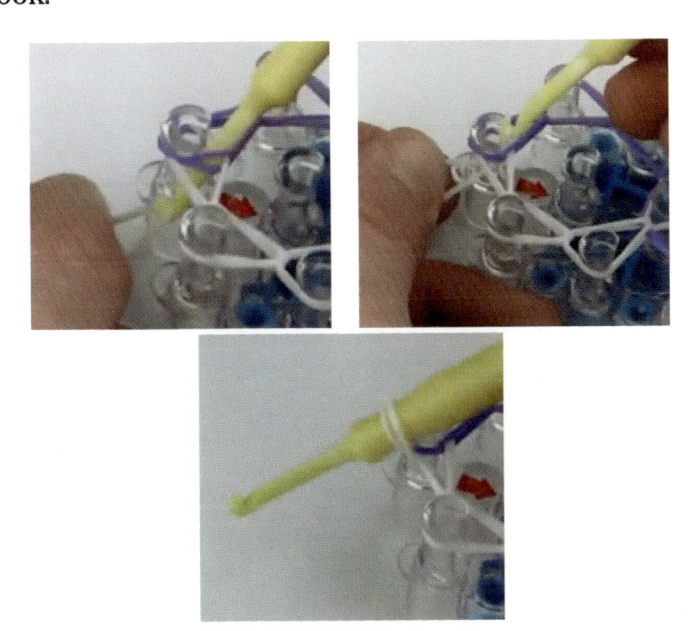

Now you can gently remove the bands from the loom.

61

Let's extend the bracelet

Turn the loom so that the arrows are pointing away from you and place a row of bands down the right side of the loom alternating colors (blue, white, blue white) Use as many as you need depending on the size you want.

Take the bracelet off the hook and grab the double white band that was attached to the hook and place it over the last pin you extended to, to the one in front.

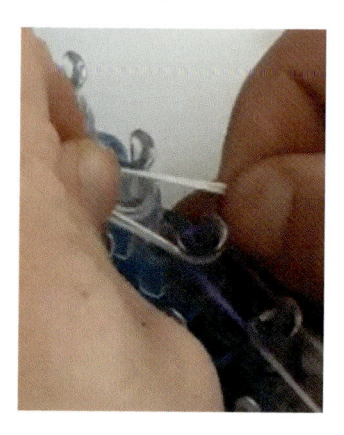

Turn the loom again so the arrows are pointing towards you and the bands are on your left. Take your hook and grab the blue band on the 2nd pin of the extension.

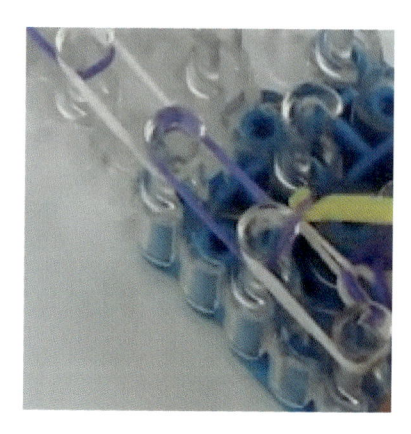

Place it on the pin in front, do the same thing at that pin and continue down the loom ending at the last pin on the left.

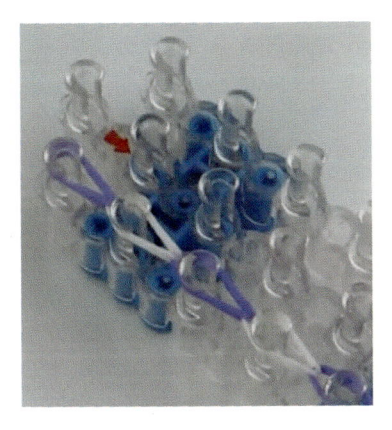

Attach a C-clip to the last band at the bottom of the extension and remove the extension while holding the C-clip.

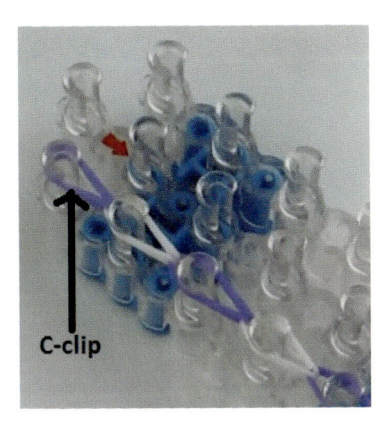

Attach the C-clip to the other end of the bracelet and……

You just made the Must-Have Honeycomb Bracelet

The Super Single Rhombus

You will need:

Loom

Hook

13 colored bands (I am using white)

12 colored bands (I am using pink)

12 colored bands (I am using orange)

White bands for the extension (0 to 8)

C-clip

Instructions:

Place the loom with the arrows facing away from you and place a white band (or your color) from the front center pin to the 1st pin on the right.

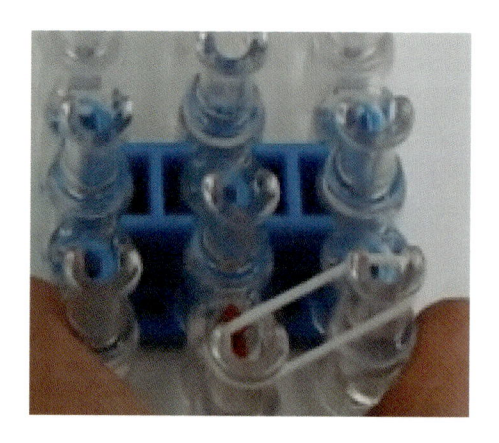

Now place an orange band from the front center pin to the 2nd center pin.

Place a pink band from 1st right to 2nd right.

Now place another white from 2nd center to 2nd right.

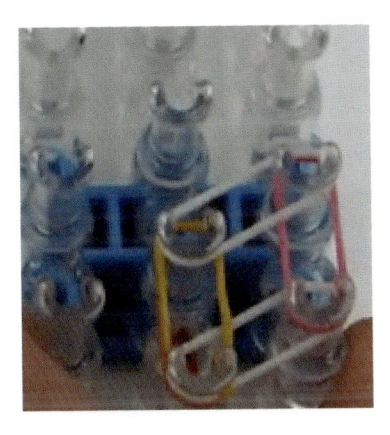

And another orange from 2nd center to 3rd center.

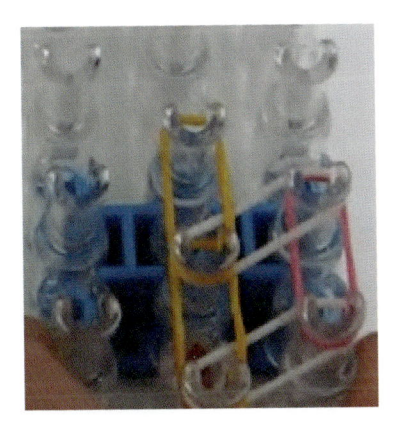

A pink from 2nd right to 3rd right.

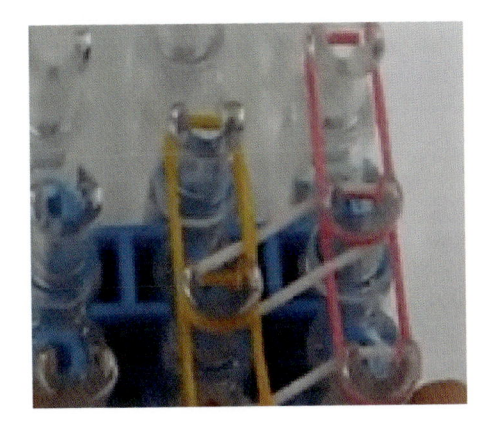

And again, a white from center to right. Continue this pattern all the way down the loom. You finish by placing a white from center to the last pin on the right.

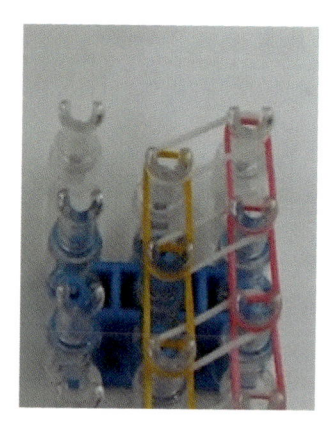

Now take a white band and double it over and place it on the last pin on the right side.

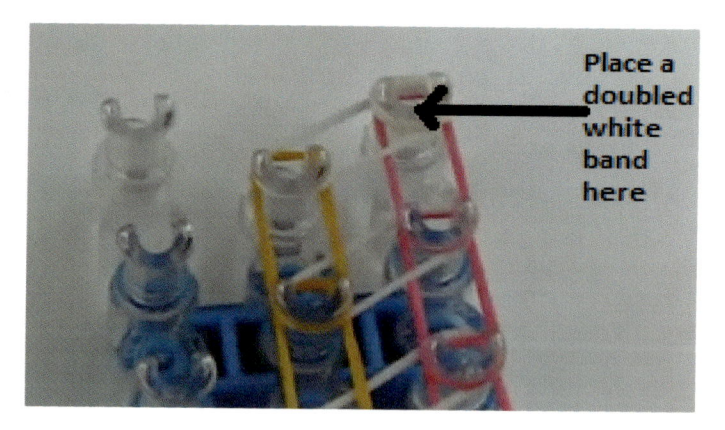

Place a doubled white band here

Turn the loom around now so that the arrows are pointing towards you.

It's time to start looping

Put your hook into the 1st left pin and grab the white band, place it on the front center pin.

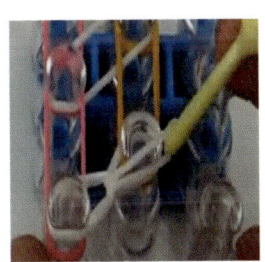

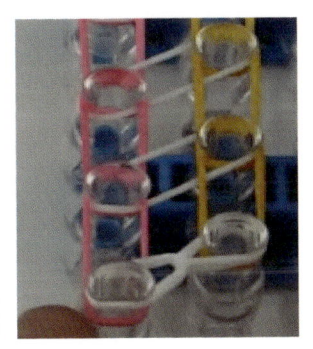

Now hook the pink band on the 1st left and place in on the pin in front.

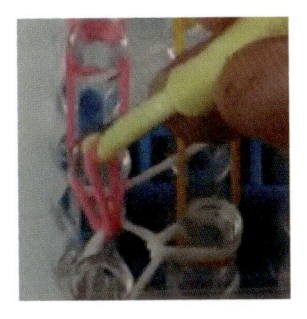

Now do the same with the orange band on the center pin.

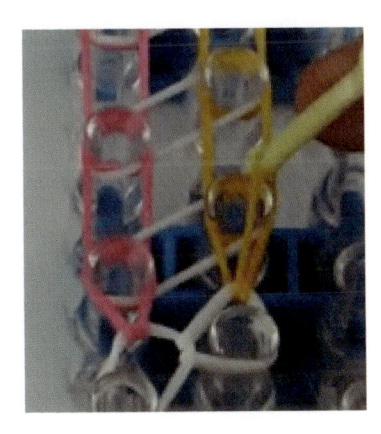

Repeat the pattern:

White band to center pin.

Pink to the pin in front.

Orange to the pin in front.

White to center.

Pink to pin in front.

Orange to pin in front.

Continue all the way down the loom and finish by taking the white band from the last right pin and putting it on the last center pin.

Now take your hook and put it through the space in the last pin on the left and out the other side.

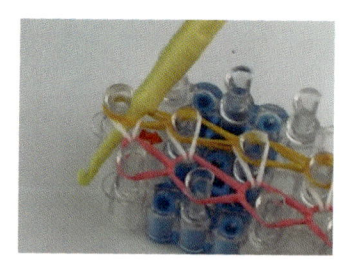

Place a white band on the end of the hook.

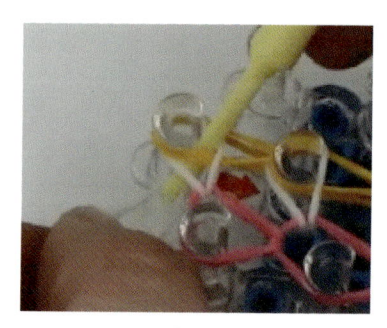

Holding the other end of the white band with your fingers, carefully pull the white band through the space. Once you have pulled the white band through, Put the band in your fingers over the end of the hook and push the band down to the thick part of the hook.

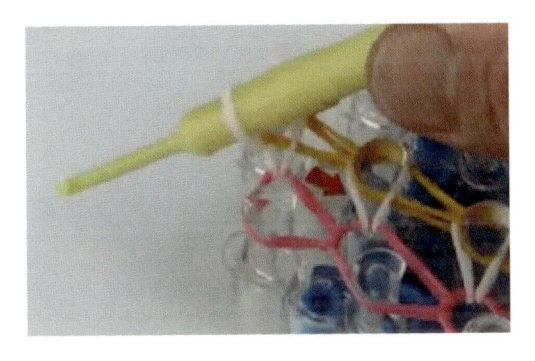

You can now remove the bracelet from the loom.

Now we can extend the bracelet

Turn the loom so that the arrows are pointing away from you and place a row of white bands down the right side of the loom (as many as you need depending on the size you want (0-8)

Take the bracelet off the hook and grab the double white band that was attached to the hook and place it over the last pin you extended to, to the one in front.

Turn the loom so that the arrows are pointing towards you.

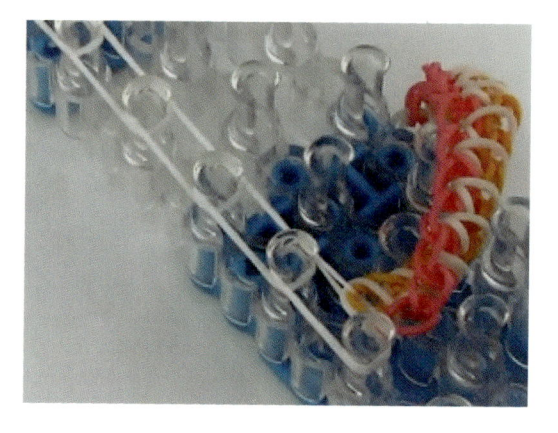

Starting at the 2nd pin on the left with a white band, grab the band and hook it onto the pin in front.

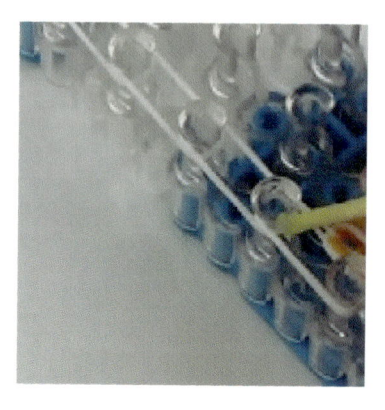

Then grab the white band from that pin and hook it onto the pin in front. Continue down to the end of the loom Attach a C-clip to the last white band.

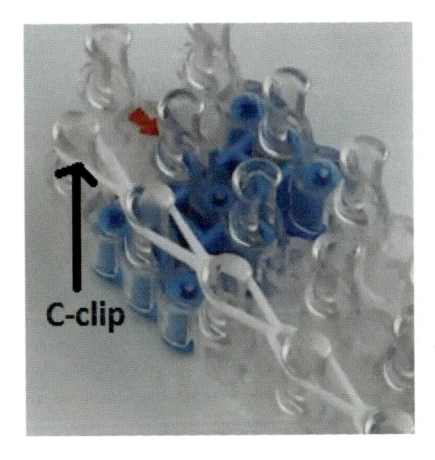

C-clip

Holding the C-clip, remove the extension from the loom and attach the double white band at other end of the bracelet to the C-clip………

....And you just made the Super Single Rhombus

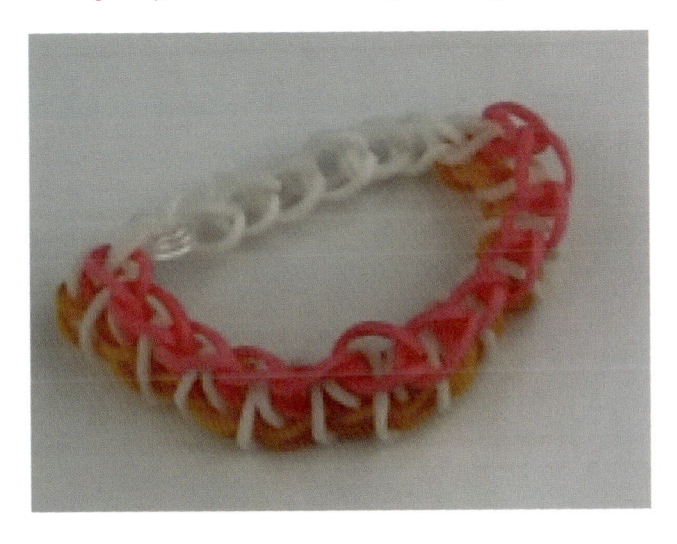

The Fishtail Friendship Necklace

You will need:

Loom

Hook

Any two color bands of your choice (I will use white and purple

C-clip

Instructions:

For this necklace, you will want to have the loom with one of the long sides facing you.

Take a white band and twist it into a figure 8 and place it between two of the pins and push it down. Now take a purple band and place it between the same two pins (do not twist into a figure 8)

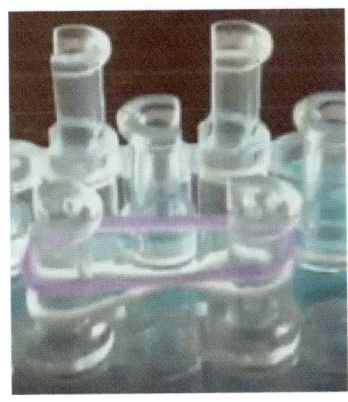

Place another white band between the two pins. Now, take your hook and from the outside of the loom, you want to grab the bottom white band and pull it up and over the left pin and let it rest in the middle between the 2 pins. Do the same on the right pin.

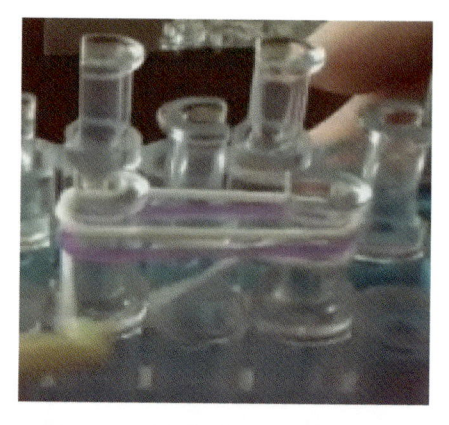

Push down all the bands, put a purple band between the 2 pins and do the same things again. Grab the band from the outside (This time you will be hooking the purple band and placing it in the middle)

Then add a white band and do it again. Continue adding white then purple then white then purple. The necklace will start to come out of the bottom so each time, gently pull it down from underneath and remember to push down the bands on the pins.

Once it gets to be as long as you want it to be, take it of the loom by holding the middle part with your finger and thumb and pull it off. Now carefully slide out the white and purple bands and discard but keep hold of the white band underneath. Attach a C-clip to both loops of this white band and then attach it to the other end of the necklace.

You have now finished the Fishtail Friendship Necklace

The Super Hip Headband

You will need::

Loom

Hook

Colored bands of your choice (I am using black and pink)

A five and a half inch piece of elastic

Another hook to hold the bands (You can also use a pencil or pen)

C-clip

A pair of scissors

Instructions:

Place the loom with the arrows pointing away from you.

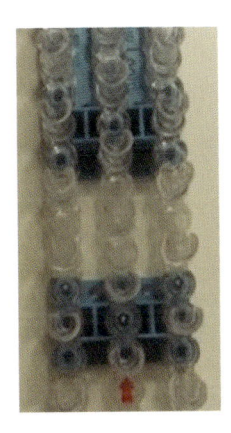

Place black bands from the 1st pin on the left all the way down to the end of the loom.

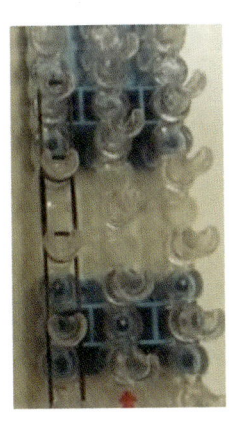

Do the same thing with the pink bands all the way down the center row of the loom

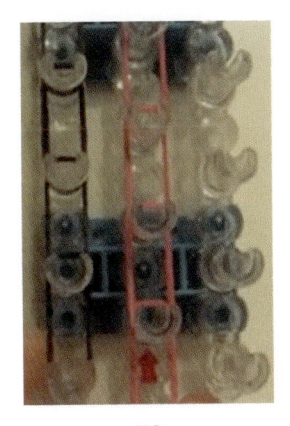

And do the same with the black bands all the way down the right side of the loom.

Now turn the loom so that the arrows are pointing towards you and place a black band in a triangle shape around the first 3 pins.

Go to the next 3 pins and do the same thing. Do this all the way down the loom but don't include the top 3 pins (where the arrow is)

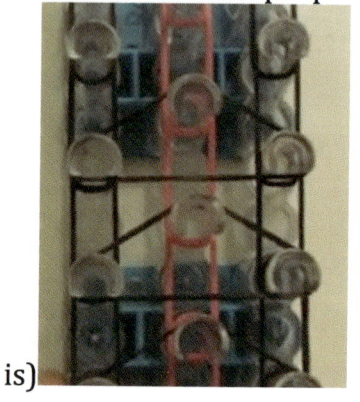

It is very important that each time you add the triangle, you push down the bands underneath (But NOT the triangle bands)

It's time to start looping

Go back to the start of the loom (arrows pointing towards you) and using your hook, push back the triangle band and grab the bottom black band on the 1st left pin and place it on the pin in front. Do this all the way down the left side. Do the same on the center row (it will be easier on the center row as you can easily see the bottom band) It should like the image below.

Continue looping down the center row and then do the same on the right row. (Again here you will have to push back the triangle bands with your loom to grab the bottom black band) (Push the triangle back, grab the bottom black band and hook it up and over onto the pin in front) Continue all the way down the right row.

Once you have completed all 3 rows of hooking, Take your spare hook (I am using a pencil) and push the end of it through the bottom right band at the end of the loom (by the arrow) and take the band off the loom and onto the pencil. Do the same at the middle and left pins

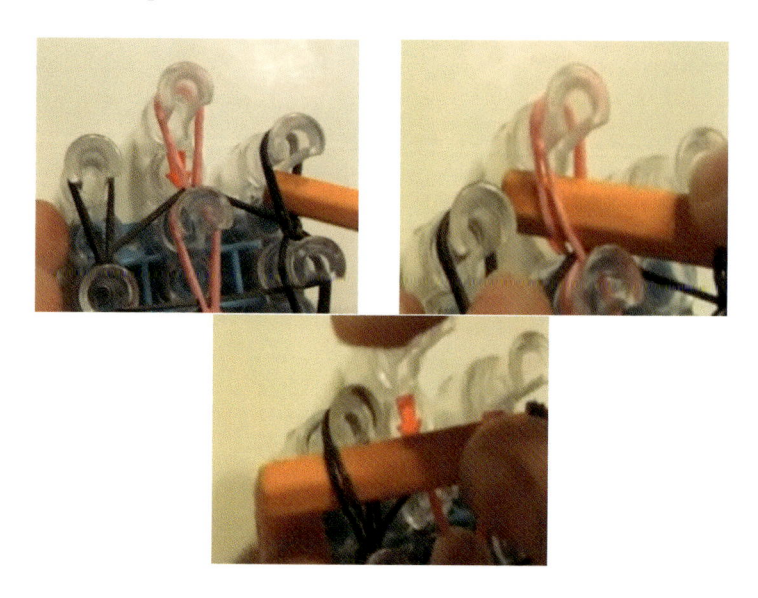

Until you have 3 bands on the pencil

Now you can carefully pull all the bands off the loom.

Time to make the extension

Now, starting at the end of the loom with the arrow pointing away from you, place a black band from front center to 1st left and one from front center to 1st right.

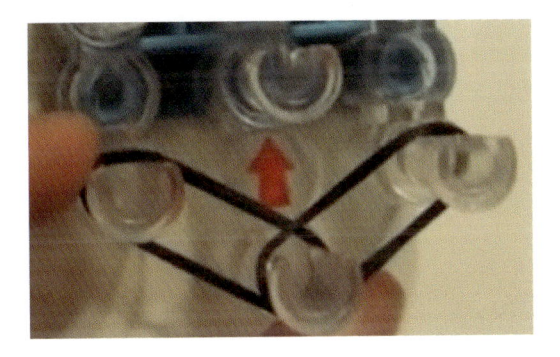

Now place black bands from the 1st pin on the left all the way down to the end of the loom. Do the same thing with the pink bands all the way down the center row of the loom, and the black all the way down the right side of the loom (just like you did in the beginning)

Turn the loom around so the arrow is pointing towards you and skipping the first 3 pins, place a black band in a triangle around the 2nd left, center and right pins.

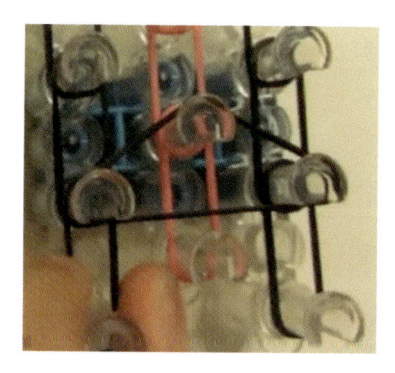

Continue placing the triangle bands all the way down to the end of the loom but do NOT do the last 3 pins.

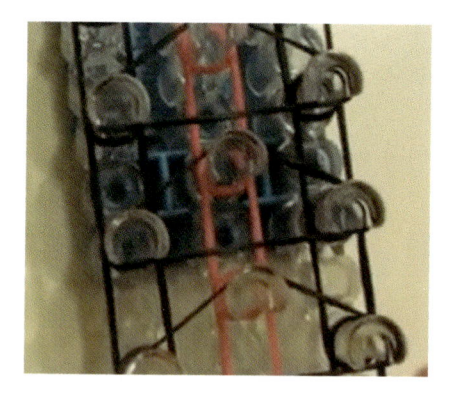

Now, making sure the arrow is pointing towards you go to the front of the loom and get your headband that is on the pencil. Carefully get the black bands from the end and put them over your fingers. The put the loop from your finger onto the front left pin. Do the same with the pink band and place that onto your fingers then on the center pin and then the last black band goes on the right pin.

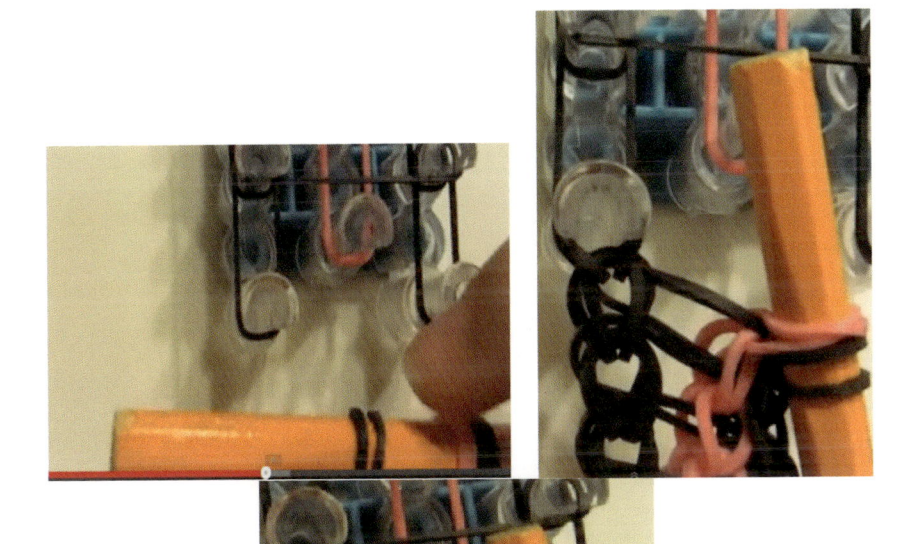

It should look like the image below.

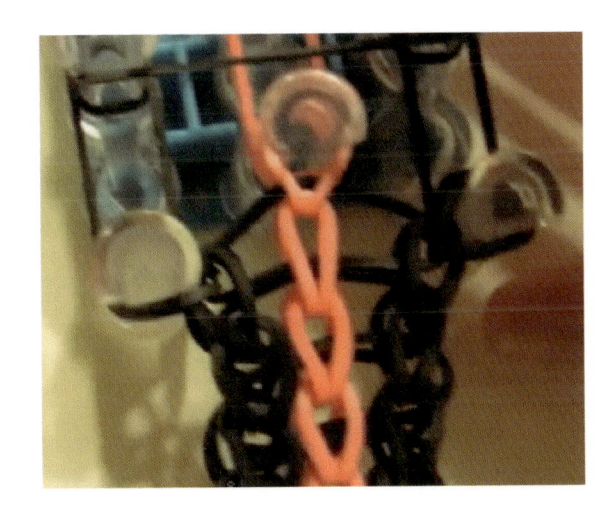

Now take the top lop from all 3 front pins (starting with the one on the right) and place them onto the pencil.

Take a black band and make the triangle again over the 1st 3 pins.

Now carefully take the loops off the pencil and put them back on the loom starting with the 1st left.

You are now ready to loop again

Put the hook into the 1st left pin and pushing back all the other bands, grab the bottom black band, pull it up and over and place it on the pin in front. Do the same on the center front pin and the left front pin.

Now go back to the left side and grab the bottom black band from the 2nd pin and place it on the pin in front. Continue all the way down the left row. Now do the same on the center row and the right row continuing all the way down the loom on these rows. At the last pin on the left and right row, you will place the bands on the center pin (Remember you are pushing back on the black triangle bands and grabbing the bottom band each time)

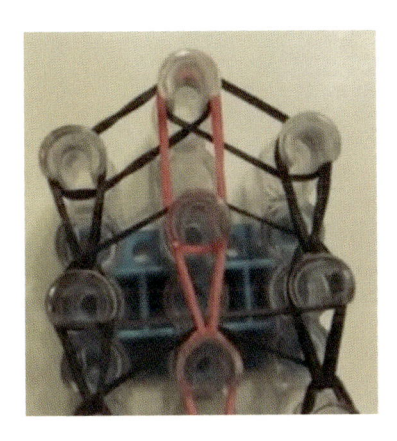

Now go to the bottom of the loom where you just finished and grab the black band from the last right pin and place it on the last center pin. Do the same on the left pin and again on the center pin.

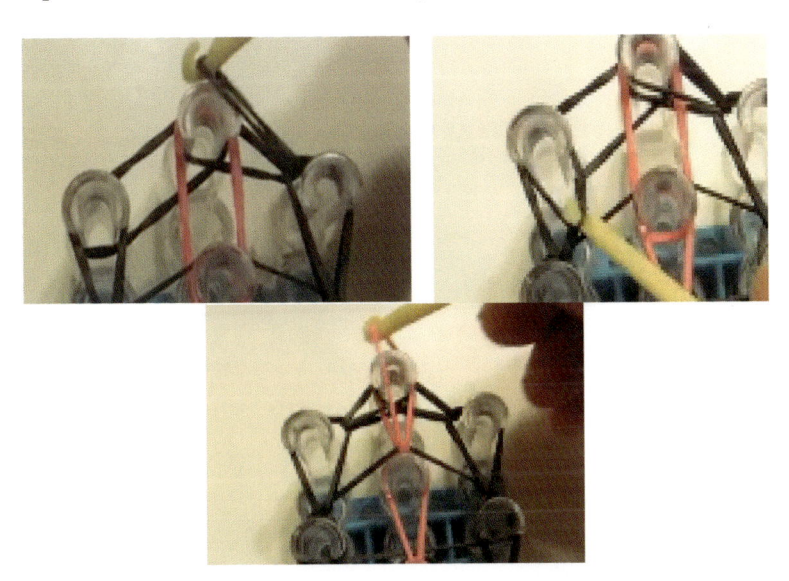

Now, put your hook into the space at the front and out of the space on the left side of the pin. Take one of your pink bands and put one end of it over the end of the hook holding the other end with your fingers then carefully pull the band through the space and put the other end of the band onto your hook. Push the bands down to the thick part of the hook

You can now carefully remove the bands from the loom. Pull at the bands a bit to adjust the headband. You will see at one end you have a big band with 6 bands wrapped around it. You are going to push your hook through those 6 bands and get them onto your hook.

Now take another pink band and holding one end with your fingers put the other end on the hook and pull it through the bands. Take the other end off your fingers and onto the hook. Push all the bands down to the thick part of the hook You can now cut the big band and pull it out. You should now have 2 pink bands on your hook (it looks like you have 4 but they are doubled)

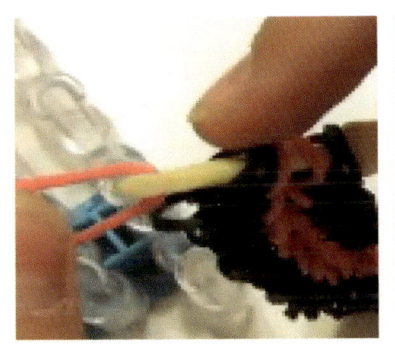

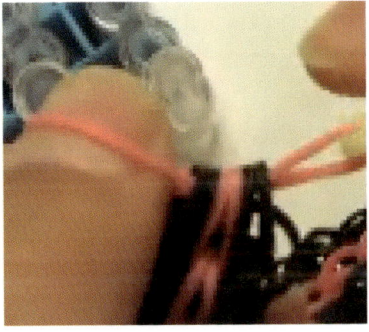

Slide the pink band that is on the left down to the end of your hook. Take another pink band from your collection and put it on the end of the hook. Put the other end of the band on your thumb and then pull the band through the band that is on the hook keeping the other end on your thumb. Then put the end from your thumb onto the hook .

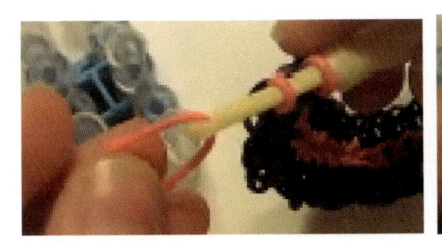

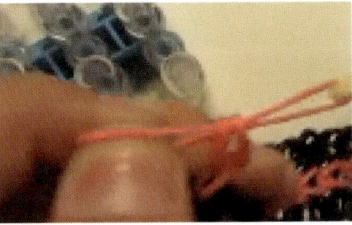

Take another pink band and repeat, take another pink band and repeat. It should start to look like the image below. Do 8 bands in total.

When you have pulled 8 pink bands through, attach a C-clip to the last pink band.

Now go to the other two bands on the hook, push them down to the end of the hook and do exactly what you just did on the other side (take a new pink band , one end on your thumb and pull the other end through then put both ends on the hook. Repeat until you have 8 bands total. (Note) If you have a bigger head, you may need more than 8 each side) Now go to the extension that you just finished and pull on the bands to make room for your finger and put your finger in the band so that you can now thread the five and a half inch piece of elastic band through the pink bands.

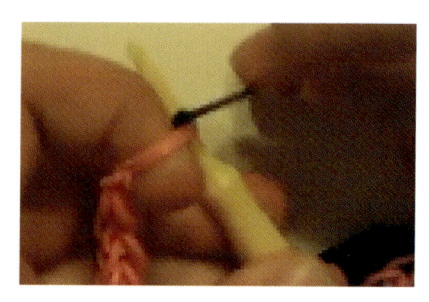

Go to the other end and take the bands off the C-clip and put them onto the hook and do the same thing (put the elastic band through the pink bands) Now tie a knot in the end of the elastic and you are done!

Congratulations. You just completed an Intermediate Loom project.

WELL DONE!

About the Author

Melinda became interested in loom jewelry when her daughter got a loom as a birthday gift last year. Since then, she and her daughter have spent many hours creating their own bracelets, headbands, earrings, key-chains and other fun and exciting things. It was her daughter's suggestion that Melinda write a "how to" book on the subject and she hopes that this beginners guide will help you on your way to creating your own jewelry and bracelets and that you will have as much fun as melinda and her daughter.

Melinda also became interested in alternative soap about 20 years ago after her son suffered from teen acne and the commercial soaps just seemed to make his condition worse. She began her search for a more natural, healthier soap for her family. She didn't realize then, just how fascinated she would become with the process of making home made soaps and how much she would love making them.

Since that time, Melinda has made hundreds of soaps and sells them at many of her local flea markets, festivals, and other local and regional events.

Melinda is an avid cook and lives with her husband, 3 children 2 dogs, a cat, and a yellow bellied turtle in Swanville, Maine

Other books by this author

Crock-pot Recipes & Slow Cooker Meals (52 Delicious Weekly Meals)

SOAP: How to Make Natural Handmade Soaps

Prep Freeze Serve: Great Tasting Meals You Can Create in Advance

CPSIA information can be obtained
at www.ICGtesting.com
Printed in the USA
LVIC04n2148200514
386677LV00013B/48